P9-DNM-134

Creation

Facts of Life

Gary Parker

Master
Books

Creation
Facts of Life

First printing: 1994
Fifth printing: March 1997
Sixth printing: February 1998

ISBN: 0-89051-200-0
Library of Congress Number: 94-96175

Cover art: Jay Wegter

Printed in the United States of America.

Table of Contents

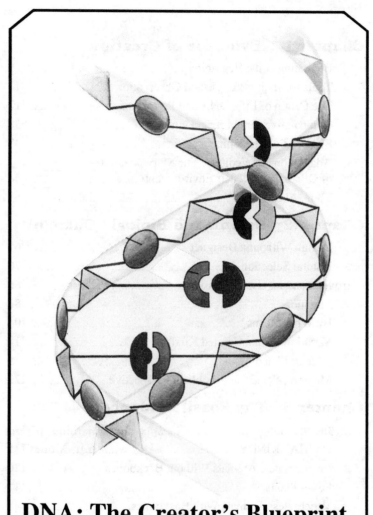

DNA: The Creator's Blueprint

Chapter 1

Evidence of Creation

Beginning at the Beginning

Did you ever come into the middle of a murder mystery or spy thriller? Some people are chasing others, shooting, ransacking hotel rooms. But you don't know what they're looking for or why. You don't even know who the "good guys" are or the "bad." Confusing and unsettling, isn't it? The only way to find out where you are in the story, and where you're going, of course, is to go back to the beginning.

Our lives are much like coming into the middle of a spy story. As soon as we're old enough to be conscious of our surroundings, we find nice people around us, some not-so-nice, and some always bickering about something that happened before we were born. In school, we learn certain nations are friends of ours, but others are enemies—but some of the ones that were enemies are now friends (and some think some of our friends are really enemies in disguise). Our parents say it's wrong; our peers say it's "cool." It's hard to figure out who the "good guys" are and who are the "bad."

We know we're supposed to be looking for something. It's got something to do with "happiness"—but what is it: Money? Success? Family? Friends? Self-sacrifice? Beating your competitors? All of these? None of these? Confusing and unsettling, isn't it?

Perhaps the only way to find out where we are in the human drama, and where we should be going, is to go back to the very beginning.

Human beginnings were once the domain of philosophers, religious leaders, college "bull sessions," park-bench debates, and barroom brawls. But now "science" has gotten into the act.

I love science! One thing that attracted me to science as a college student was simply this: Scientists get answers. In philosophy, history, and literature classes, we always seemed to be studying "age-old questions," no closer (or not even as close?) to the answers than were Plato or Aristotle. But in science classes, things were always moving forward. We found out one answer was wrong and another answer was right, and then we moved on to the next question.

Maybe, I thought, science can help us with the really big question: How did it all begin—the universe, the earth, life itself, my life? Some scientists now believe they can take us right back to the very beginning of everything!

In the beginning was hydrogen. At first that hydrogen was pressed together into some incredibly dense ball of matter. Then, for reasons we may never fully understand, that ball of matter exploded in a "Big Bang" that sent radiation, gas, and dust rushing out into the ever-expanding reaches of our universe. Under the influence of gravity, particles began to collect to form galaxies. Within those galaxies, stars began to shine. Around those stars, cold material collected to form planets. Of all the millions and billions of planets that must have formed in a manner like this, one is this tiny chunk of rock we call home, the earth.

At first the earth was quite different from what it is now. Lightning flashed back and forth in an atmosphere of methane and ammonia for perhaps a billion years, producing molecules that rained down into the ancient oceans. Then, just by chance, a group of molecules got together that could reproduce, and life on earth began.

About 600 million years ago, fossils first began to form, in abundance, of those early, simple kinds of life, forms like the trilobites. About 400 million years ago, the first land plants and animals appeared in the sequence. About four million years ago, certain apes took those first upright steps toward becoming human beings.

People are the first animals able to look back over the history of their own development. As we do so, we learn things that help us understand ourselves and our nature. Why do we do things harmful to our own kind? It's that "jungle fight for survival" that brought us into being in the first place.

But we're not without hope. We're already beginning to take control of that molecule of heredity, DNA. Using the techniques of genetic engineering, we can re-make ourselves into our own image of what mankind really ought to be. We're already reaching for the stars. There's simply no limit to what human beings can do.

Have you heard that story before? I'm sure you have. It's a story told over and over again in textbooks, television programs, museum displays, and magazines. It's a story called "evolution." It's a story I taught my students during the first several years I taught university biology.

For me, "evolution" was much more than just a scientific theory. It was a total world-and-life view, an alternate religion, a substitute for God. It gave me a feeling of my place in the universe, and a sense of my relationship to others, to society, and to the world of nature that had ultimately given me life. I knew who the "good guys" were, and where I was going.

I had heard Christians and other "religious fanatics" talk about "back to God, back to the Bible, back to this, or back to that." But for me as an evolutionist, the best was yet to come. And, as a scientist and professor of biology, I could help make it happen. By contributing to advances in science and technology, both directly and through my students, I could be part of the process of bringing "heaven on earth."

Let's face it. Evolution is an exciting and appealing idea! A lot of scientific evidence can be used to support it. Perhaps most importantly for me and many others, evolution means there is no God, no "Creator" who sets the rules. Human beings are tops. Each of us is his or her own boss. We set our own rules, our own goals. We decide what's best for us.

I didn't just believe evolution; I embraced it enthusiastically! And I taught it enthusiastically. I considered it one of my major missions as a science teacher to help my students rid themselves completely of old, "pre-scientific" superstitions, such as Christianity. In fact, I was almost fired once for teaching evolution so vigorously that I had Christian students crying in my class!

Then I got invited to a Bible study. How silly, I thought, that educated people nearing the 21st century would still study a dusty old outmoded book like the Bible. But the Bible study was led by the chemistry professor where I was teaching. More importantly, I was promised free coffee and donuts for coming. Now those are three of my favorite words: free . . . coffee . . . donuts! So, for less than honorable motives, my wife, Mary, and I set off for that Bible study. Besides, I thought, by pointing out all the obvious errors in the Bible, maybe I could convince them to study something more relevant, like evolution, for instance!

Most of the errors I tried to point out turned out to be my errors. The chemistry professor was a pretty good Bible teacher, and that got to be irritating. But the free coffee and donuts kept us coming back anyway. I soon learned, much to my amazement at first, that the Bible describes the origin and history of life on earth in a way dramatically different from evolution's story:

> In the beginning was God. With plan, purpose, and special acts of creation, God stretched out the heavens and clothed the earth with plants both "pleasant to the sight

and good for food." He created our first parents (Adam and Eve) in His own "image," placed them in paradise (Eden) to live forever, and asked only for their love and trust.

Unfortunately, our first parents sinned—rejected God's love and put their trust in their own opinions rather than God's Word. That self-centered arrogance ruined the world God had created "all very good," and brought death, disease, and disaster to the earth—a "bondage to decay."

The early earth became so filled with violence and corruption that God destroyed it in a global flood to give the world a fresh start with Noah and those with him on the Ark. Sadly, human evil has again polluted God's world, and the present world is destined for cleansing by fire. We might summarize the sad history of our planet as 3 C's: Creation, Corruption, Catastrophe.

But we're not without hope. There is a fourth "C." The same God who created us, the same God who daily cares for us, is the same God who sent His Son, Jesus Christ, to conquer sin and death and to raise us to new life, rich and abundant, now and forever. As "new creations in Christ," we wait for a "new heavens and new earth," where "the wolf and the lamb will lie down together," there will be no more pain, tears, or death, and peace and paradise will be perfectly restored.

Here's one point on which everyone can agree: Evolution and the Bible paint radically different pictures of the origin, history, and destiny of life on earth! Of course, there are many different views about both evolution and creation (which we'll discuss as we go along), and maybe it's possible to "blend the best of both." But to sharpen our understanding, we'll consider the two "classic" views of origins that have been battling it out for the last 150 years or so.

According to "classic" evolution, our universe began with a "Big Bang," a colossal explosion that scattered "dead" (non-living) matter throughout expanding space. Life on earth began purely by accident, without any plan or purpose, from a stupendously lucky clump of molecules that had the ability to reproduce. With life came struggle, and death; and those forms of life that inherited (again, by chance) traits more "fit" won the "struggle for survival," killed off the competition, and paved the way for evolutionary expansion. Finally, the sun will burn out, the universe will expand or contract itself into oblivion, and life will be no more.

In short, the evolutionary history of the universe might be pictured as four B's:

1. Big Bang
2. Big Chance
3. Big Struggle
4. Big Death

By contrast, the "classic" Biblical history of the universe might be pictured as four C's:

1. Creation
2. Corruption
3. Catastrophe
4. Christ

Creation refers to the acts by which God brought into being time, matter, energy, space, and life, all working together in a paradise of perfect peace according to His divine *plan and purpose*. *Corruption* refers to how the effects of human evil ruined God's handiwork, bringing disease, disaster, and death. *Catastrophe* refers to the worldwide Flood by which God destroyed the wickedness of the ancient world to give it a fresh start with Noah and those with him on the Ark. *Christ* is the One who conquered evil and death, and the One coming again to restore paradise, to establish life, rich and abundant, both now and forever, in the "new heavens and new earth."

What a difference! In evolutionary thinking, chance and struggle produce "new and improved" forms of life. In Biblical thinking, chance and struggle produce disease, decline, and death. Evolution begins with dead things; living things—including us—are temporary intruders in the universe, and death wins at last. The Bible begins with the life of God; death is a temporary intruder, and eternal life wins at Christ's return.

Most people agree that it's the Bible that has the happy ending: life triumphs over death. During an interview, a famous evolutionist and anti- creationist admitted that it would be nice to believe that we were especially created by a loving God who put us here to superintend the earth. But then he quickly added that it isn't right. During a television program in which I also appeared, another leading evolutionist told how he had grown up in a religious household and had heard the "wonderful story" of a beautiful creation, ruined by man's sin, restored by Christ's love. But then he went on to say that the whole of his scientific training, indeed the whole development of science during the last 200 years, had convinced him the "wonderful story" was wrong. No matter how wonderful the story, it's only self-deception (and a little stupid?) to believe it if it's not true.

That's the way I looked at it, too, for many years, including the first several years I taught university biology. But now I'm here to tell you the "wonderful story" is true after all! And it's not just me. Thousands of scientists are now telling us that the scientific evidence in God's world encourages us to believe all the wonderful promises and prospects in God's Word, the Bible.

How can that be? How can scientists—*all using the same evidence*—come up with such different ideas about what that evidence means? Hasn't "science" proved the Bible wrong? Don't we "know" that man created "God" in his image when he reached the stage of abstract thought in evolution? Wouldn't going back to believing God created man in His image bring back other superstitions and destroy the very fabric of society in our scientific age? Isn't it unconscionable (and unconstitutional) to mix religion, like the Bible, with science, like evolution?

Calm down. There really are important issues at stake here, both personal and social. But that's all the more reason to hold our emotions in check and to examine our beliefs calmly and rationally. After all, it's important to know not only what we believe but *why we believe it*. Being comfortable and confident with our beliefs means that we have honestly considered the merits of beliefs different from ours. And understanding another's beliefs helps to generate respect and compassion, even if the disagreement is deep, profound, and absolute.

This book is especially for those who love and/or respect science. In it I'd like to share with you some of the *scientific* evidence that helped to change me, as a biology professor, from an enthusiastic (even "evangelical") belief in evolution to a belief instead that the Bible is the best guide to understanding God's world and our place in His plan. But the Bible contains no *explicit* references to DNA, mutations, fossils, or Grand Canyon! My scientific *applications* of Biblical truths are no better than the evidence I use to support them.

I also want you to understand evolution clearly and thoroughly, so I'll also be going over with you—as I still do with my students—all the standard textbook arguments used in favor of evolution.

Take your time. Be critical. Think it through. It took me three years of re-examining the evidence before I gave up my deep-seated belief in evolution and concluded, like thousands of other scientists in recent times, that the Biblical framework is the more logical inference from our scientific observations.

Tools for Inquiry: Logic and Observation

Science is both a fabulous body of knowledge and a fantastic method of investigation. Most people just assume evolution can be studied scientifically—but not creation. According to a slogan popular these days, "Evolution is science, and creation is religion," and that's supposed to stop the discussion even before it starts. Let's start, then, with the most basic question of all: Is it really possible to talk honestly and fairly about *scientific* evidence of *creation*??

For many people, that question is a major stumbling block. Some even use it as an excuse to throw creation out of the courtroom or classroom without even hearing the evidence. But nothing is really easier for scientists and just "ordinary people" than finding and recognizing evidence of creation.

To illustrate, let me borrow your imagination for a moment. Imagine that you are walking along a creek on a lazy summer afternoon, idly kicking at the pebbles along the bank. Occasionally you reach down to pick up a pebble that has an unusual shape. One pebble reminds you of a cowboy boot (Fig. 1). As you roll the pebble around in your hand, you notice that the softer parts of the rock are more worn away than the harder parts, and that lines of wear follow lines of weakness in the rock. Despite some appearance of design, the boot shape of the tumbled pebble is clearly the result of time, chance, and the processes of weathering and erosion.

But then your eye spots an arrowhead lying among the pebbles (Fig. 1). Immediately it stands out as different. In the arrowhead, chip marks cut through the hard and soft parts of the rock equally, and the chip lines go both with and across

Pebble
Time and Chance:
Properties of Matter

Arrowhead
Design and Creation:
Properties of Organization

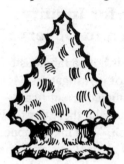

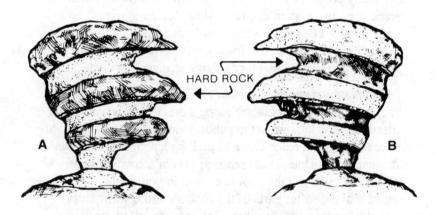

HARD ROCK

A

B

Figure 1. Try your hand at recognizing scientific evidence of creation. Both rock formations above resemble a man's head, but examine the relationship between hard and soft rock in each. Which (A or B) is more likely the result, like the tumbled pebble, of *time and chance* acting on the properties of hard and soft rock? Which is more likely the result, like the arrowhead, of plan and purpose? Can you recognize *evidence of creation* without seeing either the creator or the creative act?

lines of weakness in the rock. In the arrowhead, we see matter shaped and molded according to a plan that gives the rocky material a special purpose.

You have just done what many people dismiss as impossible. In comparing the pebble and arrowhead, you were easily able to recognize evidence of creation. I am speaking here only of human creation, of course. The arrowhead might have been carved by one of my ancestors (a Cherokee), for example. But the same approach can be used even when we don't know who or what the creative agent might have been.[1]

What does it take to recognize evidence of creation? Just the ordinary tools of science: logic and observation.

Using your knowledge of erosional processes and your observations of hard and soft rock, you were able to distinguish a result of time and chance (the tumbled pebble) from an object created with plan and purpose (the arrowhead). If we had found such objects as arrowheads on Mars, all scientists would have recognized them immediately as the products of creation, even though in that case we would have no idea who made them or how. Carl Sagan, the evolutionist of *Cosmos* television fame, wants the government to listen for signals from outer space, because he knows full well that we can tell the difference between wave patterns produced by time and chance and those sent with design and purpose.

I was in a friendly mini-debate at a California college when the evolutionist interrupted me: "But creation can't be scientific. Science deals only with things you can see and touch. Take energy, for example..." Then he stopped: "Whoops! Made a mistake, didn't I?" I hastened to agree. He and I and his students all knew that there are forms of energy, like gravity, that you can't see or touch or put in a bottle. Yet you know "gravity" is there (whatever it is!) because you can see the effects it has on matter. Similarly, God is a Spirit and can't be seen—but you can see His effects on matter. Even the

Bible tells us that "the invisible things of God are clearly seen in all the things that have been made" (Romans 1:20).

Note: You don't have to see the creator, and you don't have to see the creative act, to recognize evidence of creation. Even when we don't know who or what the creative agent is, then, there are cases where "creation" is simply the most logical inference from our scientific observations.

Although the pebble and the arrowhead are made of the same substance, they reflect two radically different kinds of order. The tumbled pebble has the kind of order that results from time and chance operating through weathering and erosion on the inherent properties of matter. Those same factors will eventually destroy not only the pebble, but also the arrowhead, which has the kind of order clearly brought into being by plan and purpose, mind acting on matter.

In a way, the tumbled pebble represents the idea of *evolution.* As I once believed and taught, evolutionists believe that life itself is the result, like the tumbled pebble, of *time, chance, and the inherent properties of matter.* The arrowhead represents the *creation* idea, that living systems have *irreducible properties of organization* that were produced, like the arrowhead, by *plan, purpose, and special acts of creation.*

In our daily experience, all of us can differentiate these two kinds of order (inherent and "exherent"). On the basis of logic and observation, for example, we recognize that wind-worn rock formations are the products of time, chance, and the inherent properties of matter. But those same techniques (logical inference from scientific observations) convince us that pottery fragments and rock carvings must be the products of plan, purpose, and acts of creation giving matter irreducible properties of organization.

Let's suppose for a moment you are willing to agree, even tentatively and reluctantly, that "creation" (the model, the process, and the products) *can* be studied scientifically. Does that mean you have to be (shudder) a "creationist?" Not at all! Indeed, there are a couple of teachers at a California university who are convinced, as I am, that creationist ideas can be tested scientifically—but they think that scientific tests have proven them false! So we can agree ahead of time that both classic models of origin can be compared on the basis of scientific merit, but that still leaves it up to me to convince you that the bulk of scientific evidence available supports the Bible, not evolution.

So far, we've only agreed to discuss, to "reason together." Now, let's apply these ordinary scientific techniques to the study of living systems. When it comes to the origin of life, which view is the more logical inference from our scientific observations? Time, chance, and the evolution of matter? Or plan, purpose, and special acts of creation?

The Origin of Life: DNA and Protein

The two basic parts of the tumbled pebble and the arrowhead we considered are hard and soft rock. Two basic parts of every living system are DNA and protein.

DNA is the famous molecule of heredity. It has been on the cover of *Time* magazine, and we often hear news stories about it. This is the molecule that gets passed down from one generation to the next. Each of us starts off as a tiny little ball about the size of a period on a printed page. In that tiny ball, there are over six feet (2m) of DNA all coiled up. All of our characteristics (height, skin color, etc.) are "spelled out" in that DNA.

What are proteins? Proteins are the molecules of structure and function. Hair is mostly protein; skin cells are packed full of proteins; the enzymes that break down food and build it up are proteins; the filaments that slide together to make muscles work are proteins.

So, DNA and protein are two basic "parts" of every living system. When you get down to a virus, that's all you find—DNA and protein. (In some viruses, RNA substitutes for DNA.) The DNA molecules code for the protein molecules that make us what we are. That same principle applies to all life forms: viruses, plants, animals, as well as human beings.

My students study all of the details,[2] but DNA and protein molecules are really quite simple in their basic structure. If you can picture a string of pearls, you can picture DNA: it is a chain of repeating units. Fig. 2-A is a diagram of a DNA molecule. The parts that look like railroad box cars are sugar and phosphate groups, and the parts that stick out from each box car in the chain are groups called *bases*.

Proteins are built in about the same way. Proteins are also chains of repeated units. As shown in Fig. 2-B, the links in protein chains are called *amino acids*. In all living things, inherited chains of DNA bases are used to line up chains of amino acids. These amino-acid chains are the protein molecules responsible for structure and function. For example, chains of several hundred DNA bases tell the cell how to make a protein called hemoglobin, and that protein functions as the oxygen carrier in red blood cells. In short form, *DNA→protein→trait*, and that relationship is the physical basis of all life on earth.

Now, what about that relationship between DNA and protein? How did it get started? Evolutionists picture a time long ago when the earth might have been quite different. They imagine that fragments of DNA and fragments of protein are produced. These molecules are supposed to "do what comes naturally" over vast periods of time. What's going to happen? Will time, chance, and chemical reactions between DNA and protein automatically produce life?

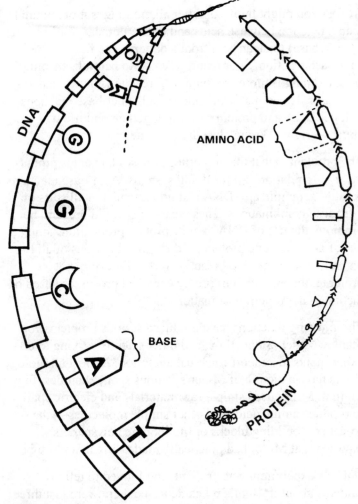

Figure 2-A. *DNA* is built like a string of pearls, whose links (specifically the *bases* G, C, A, and T) act like alphabet letters that "spell out" hereditary instructions.

Figure 2-B. *Proteins* are chains of *amino acids*. Each chain coils into a special shape that has some special function: muscle contraction, digestion, oxygen transport, holding skin together, etc.

At first you might think so. After all, nothing is more natural than a reaction between acids and bases. Perhaps you've used soda (a base) to clean acid from a battery. The fizz is an acid-base reaction. So is using "Tums" to neutralize stomach acid. Nothing is more common than reactions between acids and bases. If you just wait long enough, acid-base reactions will get DNA and protein working together, and life will appear—right? Wrong! Just the opposite.

The problem is that the properties of bases and acids produce the *wrong* relationship for living systems. Acid-base reactions would "scramble up" DNA and protein units in all sorts of "deadly" combinations. These reactions would prevent, not promote, the use of DNA to code protein production. Since use of DNA to code protein production is the basis of all life on earth, these acid-base reactions would *prevent*, not promote, the evolution of life by chemical processes based on the inherent properties of matter.

These wrong reactions have produced serious problems for Stanley Miller, Sidney Fox, and other scientists trying to do experiments to support chemical evolution. Almost all biology books have a picture of Miller's famous spark chamber (Fig. 3). In it, Miller used simple raw materials and electric sparks to produce amino acids and other simple molecules— the so-called "building blocks of life." Some newspapers reported that Miller had practically made "life in a test tube."

Miller's experiment was brilliant, and I loved to tell my students about it. But then I came to see there were just three little problems: he had the wrong starting materials, used the wrong conditions, and got the wrong results.

What do I mean by "wrong starting materials?" Miller left out oxygen. Why? Because of the scientific evidence? No. He left it out because he knew oxygen would destroy the very molecules he was trying to produce. It's hard for us to realize how "corrosive" oxygen is, since most modern living things

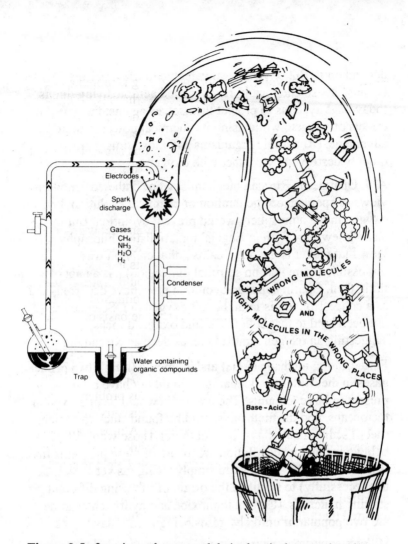

Labels within the figure:

Electrodes

Spark discharge

Gases
CH₄
NH₃
H₂O
H₂

Condenser

Trap

Water containing organic compounds

WRONG MOLECULES

RIGHT MOLECULES IN THE WRONG PLACES

AND

Base – Acid

Figure 3. Left to time, chance, and their chemical properties, the bases of DNA and amino acids of proteins would react in ways that would prevent, not promote, the evolution of life. In the same way, reactions among molecules in Miller's famous "spark chamber" would destroy any hope of producing life. Living systems must constantly repair the chemical damage done to them, and when biological order loses out to inherent chemical processes, death results—even though a dead body has all the right molecules in the right places in the right amounts at the right times (almost!)

21

depend on it. But oxygen is so valuable to life precisely because it's so chemically reactive, and aerobic living things today have systems to protect themselves against the harmful effects of oxygen, while using its chemical power to their advantage. (Anaerobic organisms and most viruses are quickly destroyed by contact with oxygen.)

A. I. Oparin, the Russian biochemist who "fathered" modern views of spontaneous generation or chemical evolution, knew oxygen in the atmosphere would prevent evolution. But he also "knew," by faith in Engels' materialistic philosophy (the view that matter is the only reality), that creation was impossible (there was no spiritual dimension). As an act of faith, then, Oparin believed evolution must have occurred, and as a concession to his faith, he left oxygen out. Science has not been kind to that belief. We find oxidized rocks, suggesting an oxygen atmosphere, as deep as we can dig.

Furthermore, methane (CH_4) and ammonia (NH_3), two prime gases in the Miller spark chamber, could *not* have been present in large amounts. The ammonia would be dissolved in the oceans, and the methane should be found stuck to ancient (deep) sedimentary clays. It's not there! Those who still believe in chemical evolution are aware of these problems (as is Miller himself), so they are simply trying (as yet unsuccessfully) to simulate the origin of life using different starting materials. (Carbon monoxide and hydrogen cyanide are two popular, if unlikely, gases being used today.)

Wrong conditions? Miller used an electric spark to get the gas molecules to combine, and that works. Problem: the same electric spark that puts amino acids together also tears them apart. And it's much better at destroying them than making them, meaning, few if any amino acids would actually accumulate in the spark chamber. Miller, a good biochemist, knew that, of course. So he used a common chemist's trick. He drew the gases out of the spark chamber and into a "trap" that would save the amino acids from destruction by the same electric spark that made them. Using product removal (the principle of LeChatelier or law of mass action) to increase yield is ordinary chemical practice,but it depends on intervention by informed intelligence. Miller was supposed to be demonstrating that the gases could make the "building blocks of life" all by themselves without any outside help, yet *his* outside, intelligent help was necessary to save the molecules from their destructive chemical fate. (Moreover, creating life in a test tube as a consequence of intelligent design would offer more support to creation than to evolution.)

Wrong results? How could that be? Miller wanted to make amino acids, and he got amino acids (along with sugars and a few other things). How could those results be wrong?

The proteins in living cells are made of just *certain kinds* of amino acids, those that are "alpha" (short) and "left-handed." Miller's "primordial soup" contained many long (beta, gamma, delta) amino acids and equal numbers of both right- and left-handed forms. Problem: just one long or right-handed amino acid inserted into a chain of short, left-handed amino acids would prevent the coiling and folding necessary for proper protein function. What Miller *actually* produced was a seething brew of potent poisons that would absolutely destroy any hope for the chemical evolution of life.

The "left-handed amino acid problem" is particularly well-known to evolutionists, and several have been trying to solve it. One brilliant researcher, after working unsuccessfully for years on the problem, just smiled and chuckled when asked about it: "Perhaps God is left-handed." He may have been closer to the truth than he realized. From what we know about the chemistry of the molecules involved, it really looks like the molecules could never put themselves together into living cells apart from the careful selection, engineering genius, and deliberate design of the Transcendent Creative Intelligence we call God!

Chemistry, then, is not our ancestor; it's our problem. When cells lose their biological order and their molecules start reacting in chemical ways, we die. A dead body contains all the molecules necessary for life and approximately the right amount of each, but we never see a "road kill" get up and walk off because sunlight energy shining on the carcass made all the molecules of life start working together again. What's lost at death are balance and biological order that otherwise use food to put us together faster than chemistry tears us apart! (See Parker,[3,4]; Bliss and Parker[5]; Wilder-Smith[6]; and Thaxton, Bradley, and Olsen[7] for details.)

Time and chance are no help to the evolutionist either, since time and chance can only act on inherent chemical properties. Trying to throw "life" on a roll of molecular dice is like trying to throw a "13" on a pair of gaming dice. It just won't work. The possibility is not there, so the probability is just plain *zero*.

The relationship between DNA and protein required for life is one that no chemist would ever suspect. It's using a series of bases (actually taken three at a time) to line up a series of R-groups (Fig. 4). R-groups are the parts of each amino acid that "stick out" along the protein chain. "R" stands for the "variable radical," and variable it is! An R-group can be acid; it can be a base; it can be a single hydrogen atom, a short chain, a long chain, a single ring, a double ring, fat-soluble, or water-soluble!

The point is this: there is no inherent chemical tendency for a series of bases (three at a time) to line up a series of R-groups in the orderly way required for life. The base/R-group relationship has to be *imposed on* matter; it has *no basis within* matter.

The relationship between hard and soft rock in the arrowhead in Fig. 1 had to be imposed from the outside. All of us could recognize that matter had been shaped and molded according

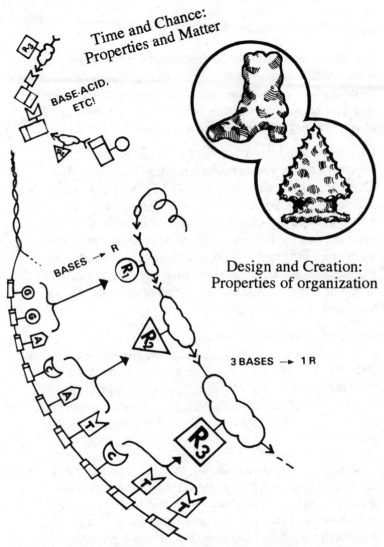

Figure 4. All living cells use groups of three DNA bases as code names for amino-acid R groups. But all known chemical reactions between these molecules (e.g., base-acid) would prevent, not promote, development of this coding relationship. Is the hereditary code, then, the logical result of time, chance, and the inherent properties of matter (like the water-worn pebble); or does it have the irreducible properties of organization (like the arrowhead) that scientists ordinarily associate with plan and purpose?

to a *design* that could not be produced by time, chance, and weathering processes acting on the hard and soft rock involved. In the same way, our *knowledge* of DNA, protein, and their chemical properties should lead us to infer that *life also is the result of plan, purpose, and special acts of creation.*

Let me use a simpler example of the same kind of reasoning. Suppose I asked you this question: "Can aluminum fly?" Think a moment. Can aluminum fly? I'm sure that sounds like a trick question. By itself, of course, aluminum can't fly. Aluminum ore in rock just sits there. A volcano may throw it, but it doesn't fly. If you pour gasoline on it, does that make it fly? Pour a little rubber on it; that doesn't make it fly either. But suppose you take that aluminum, stretch it out in a nice long tube with wings, a tail, and a few other parts. Then it flies; we call it an airplane.

Did you ever wonder what makes an airplane fly? Try a few thought experiments. Take the wings off and study them; they don't fly. Take the engines off, study them; they don't fly. Take the little man out of the cockpit, study him; he doesn't fly. Don't dwell on this the next time you're on an airplane, but an airplane is a collection of non-flying parts! Not a single part of it flies!

What does it take to make an airplane fly? The answer is something every scientist can understand and appreciate, something every scientist can work with and use to frame hypotheses and conduct experiments. What does it take to make an airplane fly? *Creative design and organization.*

Take a look at the features of a living cell diagrammed in Fig. 5. Don't worry; I am not going to say much about this diagram. Just notice the DNA molecule in the upper left circle and the protein in the lower right. What are all the rest of those strange looking things diagrammed in the cell? Those represent just a few of the molecules that a cell needs to make just one protein according to the instructions of just one DNA

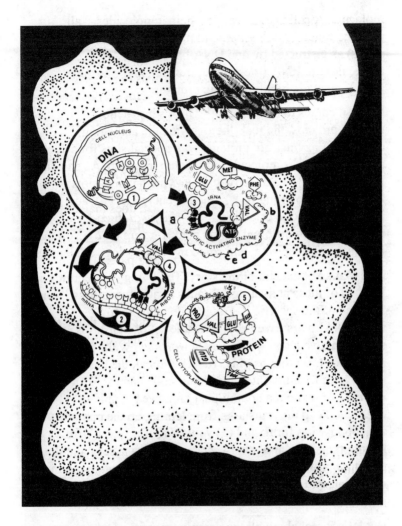

Figure 5. Living cells use over 75 special kinds of protein and RNA molecules to make one protein following DNA's instructions. What we know about airplanes convinces us that their flight is the result of creative design. What scientists know about the way living cells make protein suggests, just as clearly, that life also is the result of creative design. (Drawing after Bliss and Parker. 1979. *Origin of Life*. Master Books, Colorado Springs, Colorado.)

molecule. A cell needs over 75 "helper molecules," all working together *in harmony*, to make one protein (R-group series) as instructed by one DNA base series. A few of these molecules are RNA (messenger, transfer, and ribosomal RNA); most are highly specific proteins.[8]

When it comes to "translating" DNA's instructions for making proteins, the real "heroes" are the activating enzymes. Enzymes are proteins with special slots for selecting and holding other molecules for speedy reaction. As shown in Fig. 5 (Circle 3), each activating enzyme has five slots: two for chemical coupling (c, d), one for energy (ATP), and, most importantly, two to establish a *non-chemical* three-base "code name" for each different amino acid R-group (a, b). You may find that awe-inspiring, and so do my cell-biology students!

And that's not the end of the story. The living cell requires at least 20 of these activating enzymes I call "**translases**," one for each of the specific R-group/code name (amino acid/tRNA) pairs. Even so, the whole set of translases (100 specific active sites) would be (1) *worthless* without ribosomes (50 proteins plus rRNA) to break the base-coded message of heredity into three-letter code names; (2) *destructive* without a continuously renewed supply of ATP energy to keep the translases from tearing up the pairs they are supposed to form; and (3) *vanishing* if it weren't for having translases and other specific proteins to re-make the translase proteins that are continuously and rapidly wearing out because of the destructive effects of time and chance on protein structure!

But let's forget about all the complexity of the DNA-protein relationship and just remember two simple points. First, it takes *specific* proteins to make *specific* proteins. That may remind you of the chicken-and-egg problem: how can you get one without the other? That problem is solved, if the molecules needed for "DNA-protein translation" are produced by creation.

Second, among all the molecules that translate DNA into protein, there's not one molecule that is alive. There's not a single molecule in your body that's alive. There's not a single molecule in the living cell that's alive. A living cell is a collection of non-living molecules! What does it take to make a living cell alive? The answer is something every scientist recognizes and uses in a laboratory, something every scientist can logically infer from his observations of DNA and protein. What does it take to make a living cell alive? *Creative design and organization!*

Only creative acts could organize matter into the first living cells. *But once all the parts are in place, there is nothing "magical" or "mysterious" in the way cells make proteins. If* they are continually supplied with the right kind of energy and raw materials, and *if* all 75-plus of the RNA and protein molecules required for DNA-protein "translation" are present in the *right* places at the *right* times in the *right* amounts with the *right* structure, *then* cells make proteins by using DNA's base series (quite indirectly!) to line up amino acids at the rate of about two per second. *In ways scientists understand rather well,* it takes a living cell only about four minutes to "crank out" an average protein (500 amino acids) according to DNA specifications.

Scientists also understand how airplanes fly. For that very reason, no scientist believes that airplanes are the result of time, chance, and the properties of aluminum and other materials that make up the airplane. Flying is a property of organization, not of substance. A Boeing 747, for example, is a collection of $4\frac{1}{2}$ million non-flying parts, but thanks to design and creation (and a continuous supply of energy and of repair services!), it flies.

Similarly, "life" is a property of *organization*, not of *substance*. A living cell is a collection of several billion non-living molecules, and death results when a shortage of energy or a flaw in the operational or repair mechanisms allows inherent chemical processes to destroy its biological order.

It's what we *do know* and *can explain* about aluminum and the laws of physics that would convince us that airplanes are the products of creation, even if we never saw the acts of creation. In the same way, it's what we *do know* and *can explain* about DNA and protein and the laws of chemistry which suggests that life itself is the result of special creation.

My point is not based on design *per se*, but on the *kind of design* we observe. As creationists point out, some kinds of design, such as snowflakes and wind-worn rock formations, *do* result from time and chance—*given* the properties of the materials involved. Even complex relationships, such as the oxygen-carbon dioxide balance in a sealed aquarium, can result from organisms "doing what comes naturally," *given* the properties of living things. But just as clearly, other kinds of design, e.g., arrowheads and airplanes, are the direct result of creative design and organization giving matter properties it doesn't have and can't develop on its own. What *we know* about the DNA-protein relationship suggests that living cells have the *created kind* of design.

In the well-known *Scientific American* book, *Evolution*, Dickerson[9] seems to support my point (without meaning to, I'm sure). After describing the problems in producing the right kinds of molecules for living systems, he says that those droplets that by "sheer chance" contained the right molecules survived longer. He continues, "This is not life, but it is getting close to it. The missing ingredient is . . . "

What will he say here? The "missing ingredient" is . . . one more protein? . . . a little more DNA? . . . an energy supply? . . . the right acid-base balance? No, he says: "The missing ingredient is an orderly mechanism . . . " *An orderly mechanism*! That's what's missing—but that's what life is all about! As I stated before, life is not a property of substance; it's a property of organization. The same kind of reasoning applies to the pyramids in Egypt, for example. The pyramids are made of stone, but studying the stone does not even begin to explain how the pyramids were built. Similarly, until evolutionists begin to explain the origin of the "orderly mechanism," they have not even *begun* to talk about the origin of life.

When it comes to the evolutionary origin of that orderly mechanism, Dickerson adds, we have "no laboratory models: hence one can speculate endlessly, unfettered by inconvenient facts." With "no laboratory models" to provide data, the case for the *evolution* of life must be based on *imagination*. But, as Dickerson admits, "We [evolutionists] can only imagine what probably existed, and our imagination so far has not been very helpful."

The case for *creation*, however, is not based on imagination. Creation is based instead on *logical inference* from our *scientific observations*, and on simple acknowledgment that everyone, scientists and laymen alike, recognize that certain kinds of order imply creation.

Let me give you another example of the same sort of reasoning. Imagine that you have just finished reading a fabulous novel. Wanting to read another book like it, you exclaim to a friend, "Wow! That was quite a book. I wonder where I can get a bottle of that ink?" Of course not! You wouldn't give the ink and paper credit for writing the book. You'd praise the author, and look for another book by the same writer. By some twist of logic, though, many who read the fabulous DNA script want to give credit to the "ink (DNA base code) and paper (proteins)" for composing the code.

In a novel, the ink and paper are merely the means the author uses to express his or her thoughts. In the genetic code, the DNA bases and proteins are merely the means God uses to express His thoughts. The real credit for the message in a novel goes to the author, not the ink and paper, and the real credit for the genetic message in DNA goes to the Author of Life, the Creator, not to the creature (Romans 1:25). Creation thus stands between the classic extremes of mechanism and vitalism. Mechanists, including evolutionists, believe that both the *operation* and *origin* of living things are the results of the laws of chemistry which reflect the inherent properties of matter. Vitalists believe that both the operation and origin of living systems depend on mysterious forces that lie beyond scientific description. According to creation, living things *operate* in understandable ways that can be described in terms of scientific laws,—but, such observations include properties of organization that logically imply a created origin of life.

In this sense, the Bible proved to be, as it often has, far ahead of its time. Right down to the last century, most scientists and philosophers believed living things were made of something fundamentally different from non-living. But Genesis 1–2 tells us living things, human beings included, were just made of "dust of the ground." Indeed, scientists now recognize that living cells are composed of only a few simple elements. It's not the stuff ("dust") we're made of that makes us special; it's the *way* we're put together. It's not the metal and glass that make an airplane fly, nor the ink and paper that write a novel. Similarly, it's not the "dust" that makes life, but the way it's put together with creative design and organization. And when that organization is lost, we return to "dust," the simple elements that make us up, just as other created objects break down into their simpler parts when left to the ravages of time, chance, and chemistry.

The creationist, then, recognizes the orderliness that the vitalist doesn't see. But he doesn't limit himself to only those kinds of order that result from time, chance, and the properties of matter, as the evolutionist does. Creation introduces levels of order and organization that greatly enrich the range of explorable hypotheses and turn the study of life into a *scientist's delight*. Science requires an orderliness in nature. One of the real emotional thrills of my changing from evolution to creation was realizing both that there are many more levels of order than I had once imagined and that order in nature, and a mind in tune with it, were guaranteed by God Himself. It's no wonder that explicit Biblical faith gave initial success to the founding fathers of modern experimental science (a couple of centuries before evolution came along to shift the basis toward time and chance).

If the evidence for the creation of life is as clear as I say it is, then other scientists, even those who are evolutionists, ought to see it—and they do.

I once took my students to hear Francis Crick, who shared a Nobel prize for the discovery of DNA's structure. After explaining why life could not and did not evolve on earth, he argued instead for "directed panspermia," his belief that life reached earth in a rocket fired by intelligent life on some other planet. Crick admitted that his view only moved the creation-evolution question back to another time and place, but he argued that different conditions might have given life a chance to evolve that it did not have on earth.[10]

Creationists are pleased that Crick recognizes the same fatal flaws in chemical evolution that they have cited for years, but creationists also point out that the differences between "chemical chemistry" and "biological chemistry" are wrapped up with the fundamental nature of matter and energy and would apply on other planets as well as on earth.[11]

That opinion seems to be shared in part by the famous astronomer Sir Fred Hoyle,[12] who made the news under the heading: "There *must* be a God." Hoyle and his colleague, Chandra Wickramasinghe, independently reached that conclusion after their mathematical analyses showed that believing that life could result from time, chance, and the properties of matter was like believing that " . . . a tornado sweeping through a junk yard might assemble a Boeing 747 from the materials therein." (Remember what it takes to make an airplane *fly*?)

Drawing the logical inference from our scientific knowledge, both scientists concluded that "it becomes sensible to think that the favorable properties of physics on which life depends are in every respect *deliberate*." (Emphasis Hoyle's.) But both were surprised by their results. Hoyle called himself an agnostic, and, in the same article, Wickramasinghe said he was an atheistic Buddhist who " . . . was very strongly brainwashed to believe that science cannot be consistent with any kind of deliberate creation."

My purpose in quoting these scientists (and others later on) is not, of course, to suggest that they are creationists who would endorse all my views. Rather, it is simply to show that experts in the field, even when they have no preference for creationist thinking, at least agree with the creationists on the facts. And when people with different viewpoints agree, we can be pretty sure what the facts are. I also want to show that scientists who are not creationists are able to see that creation is a legitimate scientific concept, whose merits deserve to be compared with those of evolution.

In that light, I'd like to call your attention to a fascinating and revolutionary book, *Evolution: A Theory in Crisis*, by a prominent molecular biologist, Dr. Michael Denton.[13] In a television program we did together, and in our extensive personal conversations, Dr. Denton describes himself as a child of the secular age who desires naturalistic explanations when he can find them. But when it comes to the origin of life, Dr. Denton explains with authority and stark clarity that evolutionists are nowhere near a *naturalistic* explanation at present. After comparing the genetic programs in living things to a library of a thousand volumes encoding a billion bits of information and all the mathematically intricate algorithms for coordinating them, Dr. Denton refers to the chemical evolution scenario as "simply an affront to reason," i.e., an insult to the intelligence! (p. 351).

He openly and frankly states that the thesis of his book is "anti-evolutionary" (p. 353), but it seems to me that he is cautiously taking a step even further. The first chapter of his book is titled "Genesis Rejected," and he would react very strongly against being called a creationist, but in his honest analysis of the creation-evolution controversy through history, Dr. Denton freely admits that many of the scientific views of the early creationists have been vindicated by modern discoveries in science.

Take William Paley's classic argument that design in living things implies a Designer just as clearly as design in a watch implies a watchmaker. Denton states, "Paley was not only *right* in asserting an analogy between life and a machine, but also *remarkably prophetic* in guessing that the technological ingenuity realized in living systems is vastly in excess of anything yet accomplished by man." (Emphasis added.) Then Denton goes on to summarize his thinking on life's origin (p. 341) as follows:

> The almost irresistible force of the analogy has completely undermined the complacent assumption, prevalent in biological circles over most of the past century, that the design hypothesis can be excluded on the grounds that the notion is fundamentally a metaphysical *a priori* concept and therefore scientifically unsound. *On the contrary, the inference to design is a purely a* posteriori *induction based on a ruthlessly consistent application of the logic of analogy.* The conclusion may have religious implications, but it does not depend on religious presuppositions. (Emphasis added.)

Now that's quite an admission! Even though he would deny any leaning toward a Christian concept of creation, this leading molecular biologist sees quite plainly that a scientific concept of creation can be constructed, just as I've said, using the ordinary tools of science, logic, and observation. (In fact, Denton intimates that creation scientists have shown more respect than evolutionists for empirical evidence and a "ruthlessly consistent" application of logic!)

It's also true, as Denton concludes, that creation may have religious implications, but so does evolution, and that should not prevent our evaluating their scientific merits on the basis of logic and observation alone. Notice, I am *not* suggesting at this point that I've somehow "proved evolution is false and creation is true." Rather, I'm simply suggesting that the creation-evolution controversy, far from being a dead issue, is a live and lively question that demands serious scientific consideration.

Even *that* "simple" suggestion may prove too much for some. In what seems to me a real fear of discussing the scientific weaknesses of evolution and the scientific strengths of creation, it has become fashionable among anti-creationists to accuse creation scientists of misquoting authorities. After spending a fabulous four-hour evening with Dr. and Mrs. Denton, I then quoted him extensively in a conference (April 1987) in Sydney, Australia, which he attended and at which he spoke briefly after my presentations. Whatever others might say, at least Michael Denton doesn't believe I misquoted him! (If you're concerned about misquotation, see Dr. Gish's thorough new book documenting *evolutionists'* misquotations, *Creation Scientists Answer Their Critics*.[14])

But again, my point: I am *not* quoting Dr. Denton as if he agreed with all my thinking. On the contrary, my point is that a fellow scientist who shares *neither* my basic assumptions *nor* conclusions regarding world-and-life view, nevertheless recognizes that the concept of creation can be explained scientifically, and that the concept has at least some scientific merit.

Dr. Denton is, of course, not alone in that stand. In a short but thought-provoking article, British physicist H. S. Lipson[15] first expresses his interest in life's origin, then his feeling—quite apart from any preference for creation—that "In fact, evolution became in a sense a scientific religion; almost all scientists have accepted it and many are prepared to 'bend' their observations to fit with it."

After wondering how well evolution has stood up to scientific testing, Lipson continues: "To my mind, the theory [evolution] does not stand up at all." Then he comes to the heart of the issue: "If living matter is not, then, caused by the interplay of atoms, natural forces, and radiation [i.e., time, chance, and chemistry], how has it come into being?" After dismissing a sort of directed evolution, Lipson concludes: "I think, however, that we must go further than this and admit that the only acceptable explanation is *creation*." (Emphasis his.)

Like Hoyle and Wickramasinghe, Lipson is a bit surprised and unhappy with his own conclusion. He writes, "I know that this [creation] is anathema to physicists, as indeed it is to me, . . . " But his sense of honesty and scientific integrity forces him to conclude his sentence thus: ". . . but we must not reject a theory that we do not like if the experimental evidence supports it." That's the spirit I'd like to encourage in this book: a willingness to look openly at all sides of an issue, to draw the most logical inference from the weight of evidence, and to follow "truth" wherever it might lead, regardless of personal preference and preconceptions.

By the way, let me assure you that not *all* who see the evidence of creation are unhappy about it! Witness Dr. Dean Kenyon. Dr. Kenyon is a molecular biologist whose area of research interest is specifically the origin of life. His book on life's origin, *Biochemical Predestination*, opened with laudatory phrases for Darwinian evolution, and he taught evolution at San Francisco State University for many years.

A couple of students in Dr. Kenyon's class once asked him to read a book on creation science. He didn't want to, but, thanks to their polite persistence, he resolved to read it and refute it. But, as he told me in person, he read it and *couldn't* refute it. Instead, Dr. Kenyon got interested in creation science and began a re-evaluation of the scientific evidence, which finally led him to the happy conclusion that life, including his, is here as a result of creation, the deliberate plan and purpose of a personal Creator God! He still presents the evidence cited in favor of evolution in his classes, but he also allows his students to weigh that against the evidence that favors creation.

Like mine, Dr. Kenyon's change from evolution to creation took a long time and involved re-examination of much more than just the evidence from molecular relationships within living cells. Let's take a look now at some evidence of creation from other areas of biology.

Comparative Similarities: Homology

Look at your arm for a moment and try to picture the bones inside. There's one bone attached to the body, two bones in the forearm, a little group of wrist bones, and bones that radiate out into the fingers. As it turns out, there are many other living things that have forelimbs with a similar pattern: the foreleg of a horse or dog, the wing of a bat, and the flipper of a penguin, for example, as shown in Fig. 6. Biologists use the term "homology" for such similarities in basic structure.

Why should there be that kind of similarity? Why should a person's arm have the same kind of bone pattern as the leg of a dog and the wing of a bat? There are two basic ideas. One of these is the evolutionary idea of *descent from a common ancestor*. That idea seems to make sense, since that's the way

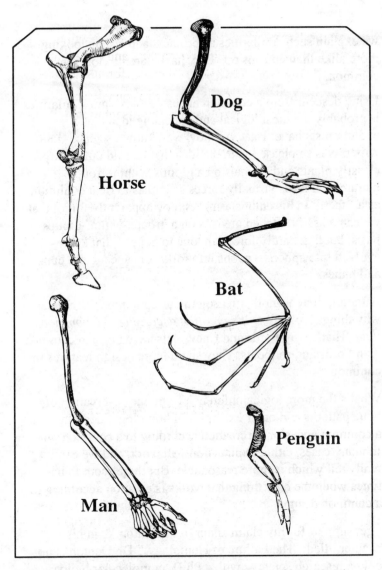

Figure 6. Bones in the human arm, the forelimbs of horses and dogs, a bat's wing, and a penguin's flipper all share a similarity in basic structural pattern called *homology*. What does this similarity (homology) mean: descent from a *common ancestor* (evolution), or creation according to a *common plan* (creation)?

we explain such similarities as brothers and sisters looking more alike than cousins do. They have parents closer in common.

Using descent from a common ancestor to explain similarities is probably the most logical and appealing idea that evolutionists have. Isaac Asimov, well known science fiction writer, was so pleased with the idea that he said our ability to classify plants and animals on a groups-within-groups hierarchical basis virtually forces scientists to treat evolution as a "fact." In his enthusiasm, Asimov apparently forgot that we can classify kitchen utensils on a groups-within-groups basis, but that hardly forces anyone to believe that knives evolved into spoons, spoons into forks, or saucers into cups and plates.

After all, there's another reason in our common experience why things look alike. It's *creation according to a common plan*. That's why Fords and Chevrolets have more in common than Fords and sailboats. They share more design features in common.

What's the more logical inference from our observation of bone patterns and other examples of homology: descent from a common ancestor, or creation according to a common plan? In many cases, either explanation will work, and we can't really tell which is more reasonable. But there seem to be times when the only thing that works is creation according to a common design.

I get support for my claim again from Denton,[16] in his chapter titled "The Failure of Homology." Dr. Denton is not only a research scientist with a Ph.D. in molecular biology, but also an M.D. with an intimate knowledge of comparative anatomy and embryology. He admits his desire to find naturalistic explanations for patterns of similarity among organisms (homology), but he also admits the failure of evolutionary explanations.

Like every other scientist, Denton recognizes the striking similarity in bone pattern evident in a comparison of vertebrate fore- and hind limbs. Yet no evolutionist, he says, claims that the hind limb evolved from the forelimb, or that hind limbs and forelimbs evolved from a common source. I was once taught to refer to corresponding parts of the male and female reproductive systems as "sexual homology." But homology, in that case, could not possibly be explained by descent from a common ancestor; we can't even imagine that males evolved from females, or vice versa, or that human beings evolved from some animal that had only one sex.

Worse yet for evolution, structures that appear homologous often develop under the control of genes that are *not* homologous. In such cases, the thesis that similar structures developed from genes modified during evolutionary descent is precisely falsified. Our observation of similarity or homology is real enough, but that's true, Denton points out, "whether the causal mechanism was Darwinian, Lamarckian, vitalistic *or even creationist.*" (Emphasis added.) Although the evidence is not as spectacular and compelling as the biomolecular data, I would say the weight of our present knowledge of homology favors Denton's final alternative: creation according to a common design.

The non-branching nature of trait distribution produces practical problems for the biologist. One of the students I taught, for example, had a passion for lizard ear bones. He came in late in the evening and early in the morning, always dissecting lizard ear bones, sectioning them, and so on. That got him interested in lizards in general. But he noted that in attempts to classify lizards, one person would go by the field characteristics, and come up with one system. Another researcher would go by the bone patterns, and come up with *another* system. Internal organs suggested a third, and so on. The pattern is not a branching one suggesting evolutionary descent from a common ancestor; rather, it is a mosaic or modular pattern (which I'll discuss further in the next chapter) suggesting creation.

Perhaps the clearest anatomical evidence of creation is "convergence." The classic example is the similarity between the eyes of humans and vertebrates and the eyes of squids and octopuses. Evolutionists recognize the similarity between the eyes easily enough, but they've never been able to find or even imagine a common ancestor with traits that would explain these similarities. So, instead of calling these eyes homologous organs, they call them examples of "convergent evolution." That really means that we have *another* example of similarity in structure that cannot be explained as evolutionary descent from a common ancestor.

"Convergence," in the sense of similar structures designed to meet similar needs, would be expected, of course, on the basis of creation according to a common design. And as we'll see later, both the octopus eye and the vertebrate eye are complete, complex, and totally distinct from one another right from their first appearance in the fossil sequence. Biologist Michael Land[17] sounds like a creationist when he mentions in passing that the vertebrate eye "shares design features but not evolution" with the eye of the cephalopod mollusks such as the octopus.

The real focus of Land's article, however, is "divergence," the occurrence of quite distinct structures in plants and animals that otherwise are supposed to be close evolutionary relatives. Certain shrimp-like animals that live in deep ocean darkness, he says, have compound eyes with lenses all arranged to focus light at a common point (rather than forming multiple images, as most compound eyes do). But, he continues, some members of the group have "lens cylinders" that smoothly bend the incoming light (because of smoothly varied refractive indices), whereas others have square facets with a "mirror system" for focus (utilizing even a double-corner bounce). Ingenious use of physics and geometry should be evidence enough of creation it seems to me—but there's more.

Comparing the mirrors with the lens cylinder system, Land says: "Both are successful and very sophisticated image-forming devices, but I cannot imagine an intermediate form [or common ancestral type] that would work at all." The kind of design in these eyes, he says, seems impossible to explain as a result of evolutionary relationship. So Land goes on to suggest that the shrimp-like animals with different systems should not be classified as evolutionary relatives, even though they are otherwise quite similar.

Even more interesting is Land's statement about how he felt when he was trying to figure out the mirror system. He said he was "trying not to come to the conclusion that these eyes had been put there by God to confuse scientists." May I suggest instead that these eyes were put there by God to *inform* scientists. As such cases show, a mind open to examples of created order can hasten and enrich the scientific search for understanding.

Some evolutionists admit they have failed to find good evidence of evolution in comparing large structures, so they are looking instead for homology among molecules. In a foundational book basically describing the three-dimensional structures first known for proteins, Dickerson and Geis[18] make the statement: "One fact . . . has emerged in the last 15 years from the perfection of protein sequence and structure analysis . . . We can pin down with great precision the relationships between the species and how the proteins evolved." Then, with every example they give, they proceed to *disprove* that evolutionary prediction.

Consider hemoglobin, for example, the protein that carries oxygen in red blood cells. Dickerson says that hemoglobins pose " . . . a puzzling problem. Hemoglobins occur sporadically among the invertebrate phyla [the animals

43

without backbones], in no obvious pattern." That is, they don't occur in an evolutionary *branching* pattern. I would suggest that they *do* occur in a creationist *mosaic* or *modular* pattern, like bits of blue-colored stone in an artist's mosaic. We find hemoglobin in nearly all vertebrates, but we also find it in some annelids (the earthworm group), some echinoderms (the starfish group), some mollusks (the clam group), some arthropods (the insect group), and even in some bacteria! In all these cases, we find the same kind of molecule—complete and fully functional. As Dickerson observes, "It is hard to see a common line of descent snaking in so unsystematic a way through so many different phyla . . . ."

If evolution were true, we ought to be able to trace how hemoglobin evolved. But we can't. Could it be *repeated* evolution, the spontaneous appearance of hemoglobin in all these different groups independently, asks Dickerson? He answers that repeated evolution seemed plausible only as long as hemoglobin was considered just red stuff that held oxygen. It does not seem possible, he says, that the entire eight-helix folded pattern appeared repeatedly by time and chance. As far as creationists are concerned, hemoglobin occurs, complete and fully functional, wherever it is appropriate in the Creator's plan, somewhat like a blue-colored tile in an artist's mosaic.

The same seems to be true for a fascinating protein called lysozyme. Lysozyme is the enzyme in tears that "bites holes" in the cell walls of bacteria so that they explode. (Listen for the "pop" on a quiet evening!) Egg whites are rich in the same enzyme, and that's what keeps eyes and egg whites from getting easily infected.

By comparing lysozyme and lactalbumin, Dickerson was hoping to "pin down with great precision" where human beings branched off the mammal line. The results are surprising. In this test, it turned out that humans are more closely related to the chicken than to any living mammal tested! Every evolutionist knows that can't be true, but how can he get around the objective evidence? In his concluding diagram, Dickerson slips in a wiggly line for rapid evolution, and that brings the whole thing back in accord with his evolutionary assumptions. But notice that his protein data, the facts that he observed, did not help him at all with his evolutionary idea.

In fact, when it comes to many of the similarities among molecules, the theory of evolution is not only weak, it has been *falsified*. That conclusion was expressed by Colin Patterson[19] of the British Museum in an address to leading evolutionists whichhe gave at the American Museum of Natural History.

Patterson first lamented that his topic, creation and evolution, had been forced on him, and then he acknowledged that he had recently been entertaining non-evolutionary or even anti-evolutionary ideas. Why? Because, he said, after twenty years of research in evolution, he asked himself to name just one thing about evolution he knew for sure—and he couldn't come up with anything! When he asked other leading evolutionists, the only thing anyone could come up with was that "convergence is everywhere. " (Remember convergence—similarity *without* common ancestry—discussed earlier?) Finally, Patterson said with dismay, he was forced to conclude that evolution is an "anti-theory" that generates "anti-knowledge"—a concept full of explanatory vocabulary that actually explains nothing and that even generates a false impression of what the facts are.

Patterson said that he finally awoke, after having been duped into taking evolutionism as revealed truth all his life, to find that evolutionary theory makes bad systematics (the science of classification). He then proceeded to examine the molecular data as a creationist would, in simple recognition that creationists produce testable hypotheses, and that now he can understand and explain what inferences creationists would draw from the data, without either agreeing or disagreeing with them. What a superb example of healthy scientific skepticism! Patterson is able to see the data regarding homology in their wholeness, and experience the unbridled freedom to wonder not only *how* but *whether* evolution occurred!

Michael Denton[20] independently reached the same kind of conclusion regarding homology and the so-called "molecular clock." After documenting the misfit of molecular data with both of two competing evolutionary views, he writes this summary (p. 306):

> The difficulties associated with attempting to explain how a family of homologous proteins could have evolved at constant rates has created chaos in evolutionary thought. *The evolutionary community has divided into two camps*—those still adhering to the *selectionist* position, and those rejecting it in favor of the *neutralist*. The devastating aspect of this controversy is that neither side can adequately account for the constancy of the rate of molecular evolution; yet *each side fatally weakens the other*. The selectionists wound the neutralists' position by pointing to the disparity in the rates of mutation per unit time, while the neutralists destroy the selectionists' position by showing how ludicrous it is to believe that selection would have caused equal rates of divergence in "junk" proteins or along phylogenetic lines so dissimilar as those of man and carp. Both sides win valid points, but in the process the credibility of the molecular clock hypothesis is severely strained and with it the *whole paradigm of evolution itself is endangered*. (Emphasis added.)

But Denton doesn't stop with these devastating anti-evolutionary comments (and a comparison of belief in molecular clocks with belief in medieval astrology!) He also describes data from molecular homology as a "biochemical echo of typology," where typology is the pre-evolutionary view of classification developed by scientists on the basis of creationist thinking.

Embryonic Development

Another marvelous reflection of creation is the astonishing process of embryonic development, including the way a human being develops in his or her mother's womb. But right at this point, evolutionists come up with one of their best-known arguments. They say, in effect, "Look, if you're talking about creation, then surely the Creator must not be very good at it, or else there wouldn't be all those mistakes in human embryonic development."

Fig. 7 shows an early stage in human development. Consider it your first "baby picture." You start off as a little round ball of unformed substance. Then gradually arms, legs, eyes, and all your other parts appear. At one month, you're not quite as charming as you're going to be, and here's where the evolutionist says: "There's no evidence of creation in the human embryo. Otherwise, why would a human being have a yolk sac like a chicken, a tail like a monkey, and gill slits like a fish. An intelligent Creator should have known that human beings don't need those things."

Well, there they are, " gill slits, yolk sac, and a tail." Why are they there? What's a creationist going to say? The evolutionist believes these structures are there only as useless leftovers or "vestiges" of our evolutionary ancestry, reminders of the times when our ancestors were only fish, reptiles, and apes.

The concept of vestigial organs even resulted in cases of "evolutionary medical malpractice." Young children once had their healthy (and helpful, disease-fighting) tonsils removed because of the widespread belief that they were only useless vestiges. That idea actually slowed down scientific research for many years. If you believe something is a useless,

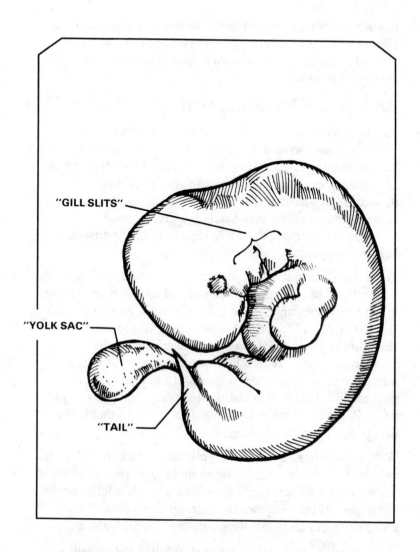

Figure 7. The marvelous development of the human embryo should make everyone a creationist, it seems to me, but evolutionists say that the so-called "gill slits, yolk sac, and tail" are useless evolutionary leftovers (vestiges) that virtually "prove" we evolved from fish, reptiles, and apes. How does a creationist respond?

non-functional leftover of evolution, then you don't bother to find out what it *does*. Fortunately, other scientists didn't take that view. Sure enough, studies have shown that essentially all 180 organs once listed as evolutionary vestiges have significant functions in human beings.

Take the yolk sac, for instance. In chickens, the yolk contains much of the food that the chick depends on for growth. But we, on the other hand, grow attached to our mothers, and they nourish us. Does that mean the yolk sac can be cut off from the human embryo because it isn't needed? Not at all. The so-called "yolk sac" is the source of the human embryo's first blood cells, and death would result without it!

Now here's an engineering problem for you. In the adult, you want to have the blood cells formed inside the bone marrow. That makes good sense, because the blood cells are very sensitive to radiation damage, and bone would offer them some protection. But you need blood in order to form the bone marrow that *later on* is going to form blood. So, where do you get the blood first? Why not use a structure similar to the yolk sac in chickens? The DNA and protein for making it are "common stock" building materials. And, since it lies conveniently outside the embryo, it can easily be discarded after it has served its temporary—but vital—function.

Notice, this is exactly what we would expect as evidence of good creative design and engineering practice. Suppose you were in the bridge-building business, and you were interviewing a couple of engineers to determine whom you wanted to hire. One person says, "Each bridge I build will be entirely different from all others." Proudly he tells you, "Each bridge will be made using different materials and different processes so that no one will ever be able to see any similarity amongthe bridges I build." How does that sound?

Now the next person comes in and says, "Well, in your yard I saw a supply of I-beams and various sizes of heavy bolts and cables. We can use those to span either a river or the San Francisco Bay. I can adapt the same parts and processes to meet a wide variety of needs. You'll be able to see a theme and a variation in my bridge building, and others can see the stamp of authorship in our work." Which would you hire?

As A. E. Wilder-Smith[21] points out, we normally recognize in human engineers the principles of creative economy and variations on a theme. That's what we see in human embryonic development. The same kind of structure that can provide food and blood cells to a chicken embryo can be used to supply blood cells (all that's needed) for a human embryo. Rather than reflecting time and chance, adapting similar structures to a variety of needs seems to reflect good principles of creative design.

The same is true of the so-called "gill slits." In the human embryo at one month, there are wrinkles in the skin where the "throat pouches" grow out. Once in a while, one of these pouches will break through, and a child will be born with a small hole in the neck. That's when we find out for sure that these structures are *not* gill slits. If the opening were really part of a gill, if it really were a "throwback to the fish stage," then there would be blood vessels all around it, as if it were going to absorb oxygen from water as a gill does. But there is no such structure in humans of any age. We simply don't have the DNA instructions for forming gills.

Unfortunately, some babies are born with three eyes or one eye. That doesn't mean, of course, that we evolved from something with one eye or three eyes. It's simply a mistake in the normal program for human development, and it emphasizes how perfect our design features and operation must be for normal life to continue.

The throat (or pharyngeal) grooves and pouches, *falsely* called "gill slits," are *not* mistakes in human development. They develop into absolutely essential parts of human anatomy. The first pouches form the palatine tonsils that help fight disease. The middle ear canals come from the second pouches, and the parathyroid and thymus glands come from the third and fourth. Without a thymus, we would lose "half" our immune systems. Without the parathyroids, we would be unable to regulate calcium balance and could not even survive. Another pouch, thought to be vestigial by evolutionists until just recently, becomes a gland that assists in calcium balance. Far from being useless evolutionary vestiges, then, these so-called "gill slits" are quite essential for distinctively human development.

As with "yolk sac," "gill slit" formation represents an ingenious and adaptable solution to a difficult engineering problem. How can a small, round egg cell be turned into an animal or human being with a digestive tube and various organs inside a body cavity? The answer is to have the little ball (or flat sheet in some organisms) "swallow itself," forming a tube which then "buds off" other tubes and pouches. The anterior pituitary, lungs, urinary bladder, and parts of the liver and pancreas develop in this way. In fish, gills develop from such processes, and in human beings, the ear canals, parathyroid, and thymus glands develop. Following DNA instructions in their respective egg cells, fish and human beings each use a similar process to develop their distinctive features. (Fig. 8.)

What about the "tail"? Some of you have heard that man has a "tail bone" (also called the sacrum and coccyx), and that the only reason we have it is to remind us that our ancestors had tails. You can test this idea yourself, although I don't recommend it. If you think the "tail bone" is useless, fall down the stairs and land on it. (Some of you may have actually done that— unintentionally, I'm sure!) What happens? You can't stand up; you can't sit down; you can't lie down; you can't roll over. You can hardly move without pain. In one sense, the sacrum and coccyx are among the most

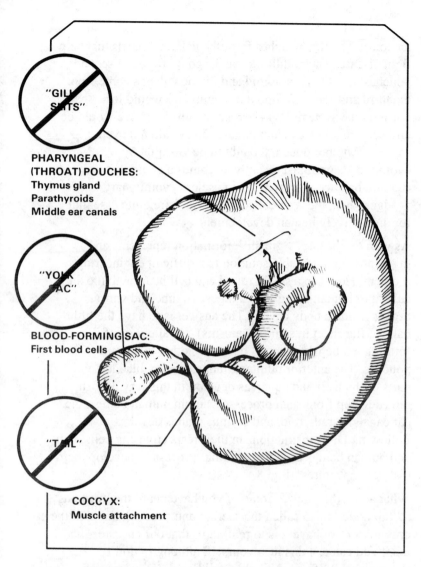

"GILL SLITS"

PHARYNGEAL
(THROAT) POUCHES:
Thymus gland
Parathyroids
Middle ear canals

"YOLK SAC"

BLOOD-FORMING SAC:
First blood cells

"TAIL"

COCCYX:
Muscle attachment

Figure 8. Far from being "useless evolutionary leftovers," the mis-named structures above are absolutely essential for normal human development. Similar structures are used for different functions in other embryos—and we normally consider variation on a theme and multiple uses for a part as evidence of good creative design.

bones in the whole body. They form an important point of muscle attachment required for our distinctive upright posture (and also for defecation, but I'll say no more about that).

So again, far from being a useless evolutionary leftover, the "tail bone" is quite important in human development. True, the end of the spine sticks out noticeably in a one-month embryo, but that's because muscles and limbs don't develop until stimulated by the spine (Fig. 8). As the legs develop, they surround and envelop the "tail bone," and it ends up inside the body.

Once in a great while a child will be born with a "tail." But is it really a tail? No, it's just a bit of skin and fat that tells us, not about evolution, but about how our nervous systems develop. The nervous system starts stretched out open on the back. During development, it rises up in ridges and rolls shut. It starts to "zipper" shut in the middle first, then it zippers toward either end. Once in a while, it doesn't go far enough, and that produces a serious defect called spina bifida. Sometimes it rolls a little too far. Then the baby will be born, *not* with a tail, but with a fatty tumor. It's just skin and a little fatty tissue, so the doctor can just cut it off. It's not at all like the tail of a cat, dog, or monkey that has muscle, bones, and nerve, so cutting it off is not complicated. (So far as I know, no one claims that proves we evolved from an animal with a fatty tumor at the end of its spine.)

Unfortunately, evolution has such a hold on our thinking that doctors hate to tell a mother if she has a baby with a "tail." They can imagine the dismay: "Oh no; I've given birth to a throwback to the monkey stage in evolution!" Then the arguments begin: "It's your side of the family." "No, it's your side!" Fortunately, the extra skin and fat is not a tail at all. The details of human development are truly amazing. We really ought to stop, take a good look at each other, and congratulate each other that we turned out as well as we did!

Evolutionists once said that human embryonic development retraced stages in our supposed evolutionary history. That idea, the now-defunct "biogenetic law," was summarized in the pithy phrase, "ontogeny recapitulates phylogeny." (Want to sound educated? Just memorize that phrase!) The phrase means that the development of the embryo is supposed to retrace the evolution of its group. As leading anti-creationist Stephen Gould[22] points out, "the theory of recapitulation . . . should be defunct today," but Dr. Down named a syndrome "Mongoloid idiocy" because he thought it represented a "throwback" to the "Mongolian stage" in human evolution.

After a university talk on creation in which I didn't mention the embryo, a student asked, "If God created us, why do human embryos have a yolk sac, gill slits, and tail?" Before I could say anything, a local professor scolded emphatically: "Sit down! Hush. We don't believe that anymore!" In a debate at the University of New Brunswick, my opponent actually complimented what I had to say about the human embryo, stressing that the "throwback theory" (based on fudged diagrams!) had been disproven over 50 years ago and desperately needed to be removed from textbooks.

It was even once believed that the fertilized egg represented our one-celled ancestors, sort of the "amoeba stage." Sure enough, we start as small, round single cells. But notice how superficial that argument is. The evolutionists were just looking at the outside appearance of the egg cell. If we look just on the outside *appearance*, then maybe we're related to a marble, a beebee, or a ball bearing—they're small, round things! An evolutionist (or anyone else) would respond, of course, "That's crazy. Those things are totally different on the *inside* from a human egg cell."

But that's exactly the point. If you take a look on the inside, the "dot" we each start from is totally different from the first cell of every other kind of life. A mouse, an elephant, and a human being are identical in size and shape at the moment of conception. Yet in terms of DNA and protein, right at conception each of these types of life is as totally different chemically as each will ever be structurally. Even by mistake, a human being can't produce gills or a tail, because we just don't have, and never had, those DNA instructions.

The human egg cell, furthermore, is not just human, but also a unique individual. Eye color, general body size, and perhaps even temperament are already present in DNA, ready to come to visible expression. *The baby before birth is not even a part of his or her mother's body.* From conception onward, we may have genes for a blood type or hair color different from our mothers'. We may be a sex different from our mothers'—about half of us are. Our uniqueness begins at conception, and blossoms continuously throughout life.

Embryonic development is not even analogous to evolution, which is meant to indicate a progressive increase in potential. The right Greek word instead would be *entelechy*, which means an unfolding of potential present right from the beginning. That's the kind of development that so clearly requires creative design. That's why evolutionists don't use the change from tadpole to frog as an example of evolution. Unlike the *supposed* evolution of fish to frog, all the genes necessary to change a tadpole into a frog are present right from the very beginning.

Again, the Bible proves to be far ahead of its time. Scientists once thought (and some claimed they saw) tiny, pre-formed people in either egg or sperm cells. But 3,000 years ago, the Psalmist, David, talked about how God beheld his "unformed substance" in the womb, and how he was "knit together," step by step, according to God's plan. His response in Psalm 139 should be ours: "I will praise You, for I am fearfully and wonderfully made."

In reviewing the decline and fall of orthodox Darwinism, John Davy[23] points out that even evolutionists see the need for "theories of *another kind*" (emphasis his) to explain both the origin and development of distinctive "building plans" among organisms. "Instead of seeing animals as collections of devices for survival, we may have to look at them as more like works of art." *Works of art*—that's the way creationists have viewed living beings all along!

Adaptation and Ecology: The Marvelous Fit of Organisms to Their Environment

We've looked now at molecules, bone patterns, and embryonic development, but the clearest and simplest evidence of creation is "the marvelous fit of living things to their environment." In the *Scientific American* book *Evolution*, Harvard evolutionist Richard Lewontin[24] says that " . . . the marvelous fit of organisms to their environment . . . was [and I say *is*] the chief evidence of a Supreme Designer." In fact, Lewontin says that organisms "appear to have been carefully and artfully designed." Lewontin himself sees it only as a tough case to be solved by evolutionary theory, but other scientists might logically infer from their observations that living things *were* "carefully and artfully designed."

There are literally thousands of examples of the unique adaptations that suit each type of organism for its special role in the web of life (Fig. 9). The fantastic features of structure, function, and behavior that make the honeybee so wondrous, for example, are familiar to almost anyone. But then there's cleaning symbiosis; the explosive chemical defense system of the bombardier beetle; the navigational skills of migrating reptiles, birds, fish, and mammals, etc. But let me single out one example for now.

Take the woodpecker, for instance.[25] Here's a bird that makes its living banging its head into trees. Whatever gave it the idea to do that in the first place? Was it frustration over losing the worm to the early bird? How did banging its head into trees increase its likelihood for survival—until *after* it had

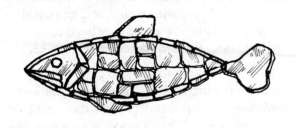

Figure 9. As evolutionist Lewontin acknowledges, living things "appear to have been carefully and artfully designed." Each type possesses various features complete and well fitted into the whole, like the tiles in an artist's mosaic. Although other animals share such adaptations with the platypus as milk glands, a leathery egg, and electric-signal sensitivity, it seems to me that all these could be put together into a single fascinating, functioning whole only by creation.

accumulated (by chance?) a thick skull with shock absorbing tissues, muscles, etc.! And what would be the survival value of all these features (and how could they build up in the population) until *after* the bird started banging its head into trees?

The woodpecker is a marvel of interdependent parts or "compound traits"—traits that depend on one another for *any* to have functional value. When a woodpecker slams its head into a tree, the deceleration experienced is many times gravity. The nerve and muscle coordination must produce a dead-on hit; a slip to one side or the other could virtually wrench the cover off the brain! The eyelids snap shut when the beak strikes its target. Some scientists say that's to keep wood chips out of the eyes; others say it's to keep the eyeballs from popping out of their sockets! Both may be right!

For such drilling, a woodpecker obviously needs a tough bill, heavy-duty skull, and shock-absorbing tissue between the two. But if the woodpecker were put together by time and chance, without any planning ahead, which part came first? Suppose, just by chance, a baby bird is born with a tough bill. It decides to try it out. WHACK! It throws its head into a tree. The bill is just fine, but it squishes in the front of its face. One dead bird, end of evolutionary story!

But maybe I got it backwards. Maybe, just by chance, a baby bird was born with a heavy-duty skull. WHACK! It throws its head into a tree. This time its skull is okay, but its bill folds up like an accordion. There's no evolutionary future in that either!

In fact, neither the tough bill nor the heavy-duty skull would have any functional survival value until both occurred together—along with the shock-absorbing tissue, nerve and muscle coordination, etc.! That's no problem if the woodpecker were put together by plan, purpose, and a special act of creation. We expect drilling tools created by people to have interdependent parts that must all be completely assembled before the machine works. That's just good sense, and good science. We would surely expect no less from the perfect devices created by God!

And there's more. Since death entered the world, some woodpeckers are doing more than just drilling holes to store acorns. They're looking for bark beetles. The beetles hear all this pounding, of course, so they just crawl further down their tunnels. To reach the beetles, the woodpecker needs more than just drilling tools; it needs a long, sticky tongue.

But if a bird gets a long, sticky tongue just by chance, what's it going to do with it? Dangling out of the bill, the tongue gets bit or even stepped on. As the bird is flying over a twig, the tongue could wrap around the twig and hang the hapless "pre-woodpecker." The answer for the woodpecker is to slip its tongue into a muscular sheath that wraps around the skull *under* the scalp and inserts into the right nostril! That makes good sense (and good science) if you're planning ahead, but poses real problems if your faith is in time and chance, trial and error. (You don't get another trial if the error is fatal!)

Evolutionists believe (like I once did) that all adaptations begin with time and chance, that is, with random changes in DNA and hereditary traits called mutations. In evolutionary theory, those chance mutations that suit an organism better to its environment are preserved by the process called natural selection. But natural selection can't act until the favored traits arise by mutation, i.e., by time and chance.

Well, what about mutations? Mutations certainly do occur, and they are responsible for perhaps 3500 hereditary defects in human beings alone. But could mutations produce the coordinated set of structural and behavioral adaptations necessary to originate the woodpecker? Let's see what two well-known evolutionary biologists have to say about that.

Nobel prize winner Albert Szent-Gyorgyi[26] writes the following about a system much simpler than the woodpecker.

He is talking only about how a young herring gull pecks at a red spot on the beak to get the adult to spit up some food (if you'll pardon the example). He says, "All this may sound very simple, but it involves a whole series of most complicated chain reactions with a horribly complex underlying nervous mechanism . . . All this had to be developed simultaneously." It's the same thing for the woodpecker. So what are the odds of getting all the random mutations required for an advantageous behavioral response at the same time? Szent-Gyorgyi says that as a random mutation, it has the probability of . . .

What will he say here? The probability of one, that is, a certainty, given natural processes like selection and vast amounts of time? Some low figure like $10^{-3,000,000}$ (odds Huxley gave *against* the evolution of the horse)? Szent-Gyorgyi says that a coordinated behavioral adaptation such as the woodpecker's drilling and probing, as "random mutation, has the probability of zero." Just zero. Nothing. Its survival value, he says, just *cannot* come about by time and chance and the process of mutation and selection.

Then Szent-Gyorgyi goes on to say, "I am unable to approach this problem without supposing an innate 'drive' in living matter to perfect itself." That innate drive he calls "syntropy," the opposite of "entropy" (the universal law of disorder). In other words, here's a brilliant scientist, and an evolutionist, whose observations of the living world force him to postulate at least an *impersonal creative force*. Here's a scientist who recognizes that creation can be logically inferred from observations of certain kinds of order, even when we don't know who or what the creative agent is.

Garrett Hardin,[27] a noted biologist and textbook author, seems to go even further than this in an old, but timeless, *Scientific American* book on adaptations and ecology, *39 Steps to Biology*. The first section, titled "Fearfully and Wonderfully Made" (a phrase from Psalm 139), describes several marvels of adaptation often used as evidence of creation. In the second section, "Nature's Challenges to evolutionary Theory," Hardin discusses other remarkable relationships which, he says, " . . . are only a few of the unsolved puzzles facing biologists who are committed to the Darwinian [evolutionary] theory." Then he openly wonders," Is the [evolutionary] framework wrong?" That is, do our observations of the living world force us, at least for the present, to rule out evolution as an explanation for origins? (Fig. 10.)

But Hardin doesn't stop there. He goes on to ask, "Was Paley right?" If you're like me, you never heard of William Paley. But Hardin explains. Paley was a thinker in the 18th century who argued that the kind of design we see in the living world points clearly to a Designer. Then, the evolutionists came along in the 19th century and argued that they could explain design on the basis of time, chance, and properties of matter that did *not* require a Designer. Now, says Hardin in the 20th century, "Was Paley right" after all? Do the kinds of design features we see in living things point clearly to a Designer? And Paley was not thinking of an "impersonal creative force" like Szent-Gyorgyi; he was thinking, instead, of a personal Creator God.

Hardin's conclusion? *"Think about it!"* (Emphasis added.)

Think About It!

"Think about it!" What a sane and yet sensational idea. What a rallying point for both creationists and evolutionists.

The Scopes trial showed it was foolish to teach only creation; is it any wiser to teach only evolution? A detailed doctoral study by Richard Bliss[28] demonstrated that students using a two-model (creation-evolution) approach to origins showed more improvement in inquiry skills than those using the now traditional evolution-only approach. (And, by the way, the two-model students learned evolution concepts better than those taught evolution only.) Furthermore, a two-model approach cannot be accused of indoctrination; can evolution only? Surely, the only way students can "think about it" is when they have access to *all* the relevant data and the true academic freedom to explore *both* models of origin.

As Garrett Hardin so perceptively observes, the challenge to evolution does not come simply from a few religious fanatics. The challenge to evolution comes from the study of nature itself: "Nature's Challenges to evolutionary Theory," he calls it. Even if various pressure groups (ironically operating under the guise of "academic freedom") succeed in censoring and suppressing all views except evolution, the case for creation will still be studied in science classes. The case for creation will be evident in sets of adaptations working together, such as we see in the woodpecker; in the growth and birth of a baby; and in the fantastic molecular integration within cells, such as the relationship between DNA and protein. Because of the way things have been made, the case for creation will always be present in the subject matter of science itself, especially in lab and field work.

We can differentiate the stone implements produced by human creative effort from those shaped by time, chance, and erosion. Similarly, we can distinguish created relationships among living things, such as those among the parts of a woodpecker, a growing baby, or a living cell.

One other special feature of creation is so obvious we often fail to notice it: its beauty. I once took my invertebrate zoology class to hear a lecture on marine life by a scientist who had just returned from a collecting trip to the Philippines. Toward the end of his lecture he described the brightly colored fish he had observed at a depth where all wavelengths of light were absorbed except for some blue. In their natural habitat, the fish could not even see their own bright colors, so what possible survival value could the genetic investment in this color have? Then he challenged the students to pose that question to their biology professors.

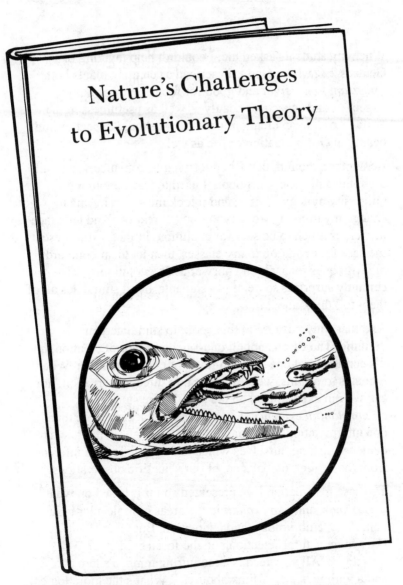

Figure 10. Marvels of adaptation are described under the heading "Nature's Challenges to Evolutionary Theory" in a *Scientific American* book edited by Garrett Hardin. Even though he's an evolutionist, Hardin asks, "Is the [evolutionary] framework wrong?" Then he goes on to ask, "Was Paley right?" when he said the kind of design we see in the living world requires a Designer. Then, in an expression of open-ended fairness that everyone can appreciate, Hardin concludes, "Think about it!" *Think about it.*

When my students asked me, I couldn't help thinking of Genesis 2:9, where God is described as creating plants both *"pleasant to the sight* and good for food." We normally expect to find aspects of beauty as well as usefulness in the artifacts of human creation; perhaps we should expect to find beauty in God's creation of life as well.

Remember, though, that I'm not trying to convince you of all these things in one short book. I used to teach evolution in university biology classes, and it took me several years to change my thinking from evolution to creation. And let's face it, there is much to be said for evolution. In fact, I still present the case for evolution to my classes, then let them bombard me with questions which I answer as an evolutionist. That certainly surprises some of my students, but it stimulates all of them to "think about it."

And that's my purpose in this book: to stimulate your thinking. The case is not all one-sided in favor of creation, but it's certainly not one-sided in favor of evolution either. When it comes to origins, we can't appeal to direct observation, nor can we run experiments on the past. We're stuck with *circumstantial evidence*, i.e., evidence subject to more than one interpretation. Our goal must be to weigh *all* the relevant evidence, asking ourselves which is the more logical inference from the weight, on balance, of our scientific observations.

The case for creation I've presented so far is based on what we *do know* and *can explain* in the areas of molecular biology, homology, embryology, and adaptation. But what about Darwinian natural selection and the fossil evidence? Well, let's dig in. All you need is an inquiring mind, a sharp eye, and a willing heart. "Think about it!" What's the more logical inference from our scientific observations of genetics and the fossil evidence: time, chance, and the evolution of matter, *or* plan, purpose, and irreducible properties of organization pointing to special acts of creation?

End Notes

1   Parker, Gary E. "Clarifying Creation-Evolution," *American Biology Teacher*. April, 1977 (Letter to the Editor p. 247).

2   Parker, Gary E., W. Ann Reynolds, and Rex Reynolds. *DNA: The Key to Life*. Rev. ed. Programmed Biology Series. Chicago: Educational Methods, Inc. 1977.

3   Parker, Gary E. "The Origin of Life on Earth." *Creation Science Research Quarterly*, September 1970.

4   Parker, Gary E., and Thomas R. Mertens. *Life's Basis: Biomolecules*. New York: John Wiley and Sons. 1977. (Available in Spanish as *Biomoleculas: Basa de la Vida*.)

5   Bliss, Richard B., and Gary E. Parker. *Origin of Life*.. Colorado Springs: Master Books. Two Models Creation-Evolution Series 1994.

6   Wilder-Smith, A. E. *The Natural Sciences Know Nothing of Evolution*. Colorado Springs: Master Books. 1981.

7   Thaxton, Charles, Walter Bradley, and Roger Olsen. *The Mystery of Life's Origin: Reassessing Current Theories*. New York: Philosophical Library. 1984.

8   See references 2, 4, 5, and 7 above for details.

9   Dickerson, Richard E. "Chemical Evolution and the Origin of Life." *Scientific American* (and Scientific American book, *Evolution*). September 1978.

10 Crick, Francis. "The Seeds of Life." *Discover*, October 1981.

11 Parker, Gary E. "The Origin of Life on Earth." *Creation Science Research Quarterly*, September 1970.

12 Hoyle, Sir Fred, and Chandra Wickramasinghe. As quoted in "There *Must* Be a God." *Daily Express*, August 14, 1981; and "Hoyle on Evolution." *Nature*, November 12, 1981.

13 Denton, Michael. *Evolution: A Theory in Crisis*. London: Burnett Books. 1985. 368 pages.

14 Gish, Duane T. *Creation Scientists Answer Their Critics*.. Colorado Springs: Master Books. 1993. 451 pp.

15 Lipson, H. S. "A Physicist Looks at Evolution." *Physics Bulletin*, May 1980. Page 138.

16 Denton, Michael. *Evolution: A Theory in Crisis*. London: Burnett Books. 1985. Chapter 7.

17 Land, Michael. "Nature as an Optical Engineer." *New Scientist,* October 4, 1979.

18 Dickerson, Richard E., and Irving Geis. *The Structure and Action of Proteins.* New York: Harper and Row. 1969.

19 Patterson, Colin. Address at American Museum of Natural History, New York, 5 November 1981. (Summarized by Gary Parker and Luther Sunderland in *Acts and Facts* , Impact No. 108, Institute for Creation Research, El Cajon, CA. December 1982.)

20 Denton, Michael. *Evolution: A Theory in Crisis.* London: Burnett Books. 1985. page 306.

21 Wilder-Smith, A. E. *The Natural Sciences Know Nothing of Evolution..* Colorado Springs: Master Books. 1981.

22 Gould, Stephen Jay. "Dr. Down's Syndrome." *Natural History,* April 1980.

23 Davy, John. "Once Upon a Time." *Observer-Review,* London: August 16, 1981.

24 Lewontin, Richard C. "Adaptation." *Scientific American* (and *Scientific American book. Evolution*), September 1978.

25 Bliss, Richard B. *The Strange Case of the Woodpecker.* Colorado Springs: Master Books Video. 1985.

26 Szent-Gyorgyi, Albert. "Drive in Living matter to Perfect Itself." *Synthesis I* (1), 1977.

27 Hardin, Garrett. *39 Steps to Biology.* A *Scientific American* book. San Francisco: W. H. Freeman and Co. 1968.

28 Bliss, Richard B. *A Comparison of Two Approaches to the Teaching of Origins of Living Things to High School Biology Students in Racine, Wisconsin.* Dissertation. University of Sarasota (ERIC Ed 152 568), 1979. See also, R. B. Bliss. "A Comparison of Students Studying the Origin of Life from a Two-Model Approach vs. Those Studying from a Single-Model Approach." *Acts and Facts,* Impact No. 60, June 1978.

Chapter 2

Darwin and Biologic Change

Design Without a Designer

"Wait a minute! Stop! Let's come to our senses! I just read through a whole bunch of evidence for 'creation,' evidence that's supposed to convince me that this world was created by the all-loving, all-powerful God of the Bible. But just look around. The world's a mess! People are starving, babies are born deformed, disease kills millions, and 'acts of God' like earthquakes, fires, and floods have killed millions more. This is supposed to convince me the world was made by an *all-wise Creator*?"

Have such troubling thoughts crossed your mind? They certainly troubled a young amateur naturalist as he sailed around the world on the *H.M.S. Beagle* back in the 1830's. Charles Darwin was brought up in an England that at least paid lip service to the Bible and creationist thinking, and his only formal college training was in theology. Yet, everywhere he looked, as he collected specimens for the *Beagle*, he found only struggle and death. On the Galapagos Islands, he watched in horror as baby turtles burst from their sandy nests and made a mad dash for the ocean, only to have their brief lives swallowed by hordes of birds or, for the very few that even got to taste the sea, large fish and other predators.

How could such wholesale waste, violence, and death result from the plan, purpose, and direct creative acts of God? Darwin began to look for another explanation for the origin of life—and he found it. After years of thought, research, and self-doubt, Darwin was coaxed into publishing his revolutionary new theory in 1859: *On the Origin of Species by*

Means of Natural Selection, or The Preservation of Favoured Races in the Struggle for Life.

Darwin's book (*Origin of Species* for short) has been claimed to be second only to the Bible in its influence on human history, and some would now put it first. Many saw in natural selection a means to explain all appearance of design without any reference to a Designer, and many more seized on that as an excuse to disbelieve a "Creator God" and to get out from under the oppressive rules of organized religion. The old creationist argument from design, "the watch implies a watchmaker," was dead; long live the new "blind watchmaker," natural selection: evolution by time, chance, and the struggle for survival!

After biologist Michael Denton identified himself on television[1] as a skeptic regarding *both* creation and evolution, the interviewer asked him what he thought the chief impact of Darwin's book had been. After a pause, Denton replied that its chief impact had been to make atheism possible, or at least respectable. The much-admired historian and philosopher Will Durant[2] said that we are now coming out of a pagan era that began in 1859 with Darwin's *Origin*. Darwin's book changed the whole course of history. Certainly, I can claim scientific evidence supports the Biblical framework for origins *if and only if* I can deal fairly and honestly with natural selection.

Natural Selection

In spite of its revolutionary philosophic impact, Darwin's concept of natural selection is quite easy to understand (*and* to misunderstand). It was based on observations of artificial selection, the results of selective breeding by farmers and animal fanciers. Darwin, for example, referred to all the different breeds of pigeons that had been produced by artificial selection. The ordinary one in Fig. 11 is the wild rock pigeon, the one you often find around city statues and country barns. But all the other birds pictured are just pigeons,

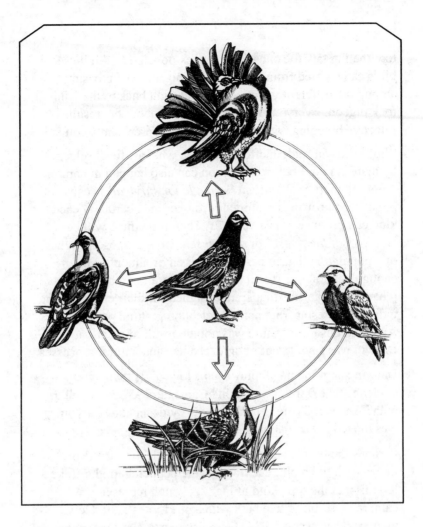

Figure 11. By artificial selection, all the "fancy" varieties of pigeons above have been bred *from* the common wild rock pigeon, and they can be bred *back* to the wild rock pigeon (just as special varieties of dogs and cats can be bred from and to the "mongrel" types). Darwin used *artificial selection*, selective breeding by man, as a model for *natural selection*, survival of the fittest selected by nature in the struggle for life. But does natural selection lead to evolution, or point back to the Biblical concept of a corrupted creation?

too: the fan tail, the one with the neck pouch, etc. All these birds can be bred from the wild rock pigeon, and crossing among the different varieties can lead right back to the wild rock pigeon. Everyone knows, of course, about the results of selective breeding with dogs, cats, cattle, roses, and so on.

"So," Darwin said, in effect, "we see what artificial selection by man can do. I believe selection can also happen in nature. After all, there is a constant *'struggle for survival'* because of population growth and limited resources, and certainly each kind can produce many *varieties*. Therefore, there will be *'survival of the fittest,'* or *natural selection*, of those varieties of a population that fit best into their environments. Given enough generations [time] and the right trait combinations [chance], organisms that seem designed for their environment will simply result from natural selection [natural processes]." Apparent design in nature was not the result of creation, Darwin was saying, but of time, chance, and natural processes.

Darwin's argument certainly seems logical. Is there any evidence that Darwin was right? Can nature select as well as man? Answer: There is considerable evidence that Darwin was indeed *correct* about natural selection.

Perhaps the best example of Darwinian selection is the one that's in all the biology textbooks: the peppered moths. Take a look first at the top photo in Fig. 12, which represents a camera close-up of tree bark with some moths on it. How many moths do you see? One is easy to see, and most people see two. (Some claim to see three, but I've never found the third!) At least we can agree that one moth stands out and one is camouflaged. Presumably that's the way birds saw it, too, back in the 1850's. The darker moth stood out, but the lighter one was camouflaged against the mottled gray lichen that encrusted the trees back then. As a result, birds ate mostly dark moths and light moths made up over 98% of the population.

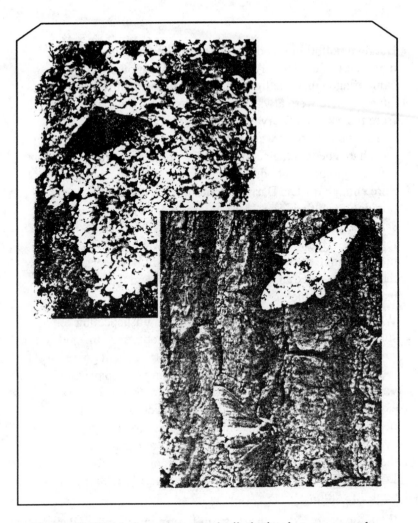

Figure 12. "Evolution going on today": that's what many people believe, and I once taught, about the peppered moth. Because of a change in the color of their background, the light moths so common in 1850 (well-camouflaged in the top photo) lost out in the struggle for life to the more "fit" variety (camouflaged by the dark background in the bottom photo). By 1950, most of the moths were the dark (melanic) variety. Can you accept that as "proof of evolution," or do you wonder if there are *boundary conditions* that *limit* the amount of change natural selection can produce?

But then pollution killed the lichen on the trees, revealing the dark color of the bark. As a result, the dark moths were more camouflaged than the light ones. The moths themselves didn't change; there were always dark moths and always light moths from the earliest observations. But the environment changed, and so the dark ones were better camouflaged. Thus, the dark ones had a better chance of surviving and leaving more offspring to grow into dark moths in succeeding generations. Sure enough, just as Darwin would have predicted, the population shifted. The "dark environment" just *naturally selected* the dark moths as more likely to survive and reproduce. By the 1950's the population was over 98% dark, proof positive of "evolution going on today." At least, that's the way it's stated in many biology books, and that's what I used to tell my biology students.

When I was an evolutionist, sometimes an unsuspecting student (often a "religious type"!) would approach me and say, "Look, if evolution is true, why don't we see it going on today?" And I would say, "Evolution going on today? Glad you brought that up! It just so happens that we have a perfect example of evolution in action." Then I would launch into the peppered-moth story. Those moths are *the* showcase for evolution. Over twenty years after they first became famous, they were chosen, for example, as the frontispiece for Lewontin's article on adaptation in the *Scientific American* book *Evolution*.

Well, the peppered moths *do* seem to provide strong evidence of natural selection. But is that evidence of evolution? Notice, I've changed the question. That's a key point. First, I asked if there was any evidence that Darwin was correct about natural selection. The answer quite simply is, "Yes, there is." But *now* I'm asking a radically different question, "Is there any evidence for *evolution*?" Many people say, "Isn't that the same question? Aren't natural selection and evolution the same thing?" Answer: No, absolutely not!

When someone asks if I believe in evolution, I'll often say, "Why, yes, no, no, yes, no." The answer really depends on what the person means by evolution. In one sense, evolution means "change." Do I believe in change? Yes, indeed—I've got some in my pocket! But change isn't the real question, of course. Change is just as much a part of the creation model as the evolution model. The question is, *what kind of change* do we see: change only within kind (creation), or change also from one kind to others (evolution)?

Take a look again at the peppered-moth example (Fig. 12). What did we start with? Dark and light varieties of the peppered moth, species *Biston betularia*. After 100 years of natural selection, what did we end up with? Dark and light varieties of the peppered moth, species *Biston betularia*. All that changed was the percentage of moths in the two categories: that is, just variation within kind. (For details, see the master's thesis by one of my students, Chris Osborne.[3])

According to the Biblical framework of history, struggle and death began when man's rebellion ruined God's perfect creation. Natural selection is just one of the processes that operates in our present *corrupted* world to insure that the created kinds can indeed spread throughout the earth in all its ecologic and geographic variety (often, nowadays, in spite of human pollution).

As a matter of fact, 24 years before Darwin's Origin, a scientist named Edward Blyth published the concept of natural selection in the Biblical context of corrupted creation. He saw it as a process that adapted varieties of the created kinds to changing environments after sin brought death into God's world. A book reviewer once asked, rather naively, if creationists could accept the concept of natural selection. The answer is, "Of course. *We* thought of it first."

But if natural selection is such a profound idea, and Blyth published it before Darwin, then why isn't Blyth's name a household word? Perhaps because he was a creationist. It was not the *scientific* applications of natural selection that attracted attention in 1859; it was its presumed *philosophic* and *religious* implications.

Evolutionists were not content to treat natural selection as simply an observable ecological process. Darwin himself was a cautious scientist, painstaking in his work. But others, especially T. H. Huxley and Herbert Spencer, insisted on making natural selection the touchstone of a new religion, a "religion without revelation," as Julian Huxley later called it. For them, as for many others, the real significance of the *Darwinian revolution* was *religious* and *philosophic*, not scientific. These early evolutionists were basically anti-creationists who wanted to explain design without a Designer.

But in spite of what might be claimed, natural selection has been observed to produce only variation within kind, merely shifts in populations, for example, of moths to greater percentages of darker moths, of flies resistant to DDT, or of bacteria resistant to antibiotics. But evolution means more than change from moth to moth, fly to fly, or bacterium to bacterium. Any real evolution, "mega- or macro-" evolution, means change from one kind to another: "Fish to Philosopher," as the title of Homer Smith's book puts it, or "Molecules to Man," the subtitle of the government-funded BSCS "blue-version" high-school biology textbook.

Still, I must admit that there is a potential connection between observed natural selection within kind and *hypothetical* evolution from one kind to another. That connection is called *"extrapolation,"* following a trend to its logical conclusion. Scientists extrapolate from population records, for example, to predict changes in the world population. If world population growth continues at the rate observed in the '60's, statisticians said, then the world population by 2000A.D. would be over 6 billion. Similarly, if natural selection continues over very long periods of time, evolutionists say, the same process that changes moths from mostly light to mostly dark forms will gradually change fish to philosophers or molecules to man.

Now there's nothing wrong with extrapolation in principle. But there are things to watch for in practice. For example, simple extrapolation would suggest a population of a "zillion" by 3000A.D. But, of course, there will come a point when the earth is simply not big enough to support any more people. In other words, there are *limits*, or *boundary conditions*, to logical extrapolation.

Consider my jogging (or should I say "slogging") times. Starting years ago at an embarrassing 12 minutes per mile, I knocked a minute off each week: a mile in 11 minutes, then 10, 9, 8, 7, 6, 5, 4, 3, 2, 1. Wait a minute! As you well know, I reached my limit long before the one-minute mile! (Just where, I'll keep secret!) This is an embarrassing example, but it makes an important point: no scientist would consider extrapolation without also considering the logical limits or boundary conditions of that extrapolation.

Evolutionists are aware of the problem. In their classic textbook, *Evolution*, the late Theodosius Dobzhansky[4] and three other famous evolutionists distinguish between *SUBspeciation* and *TRANSspeciation*. "Sub" is essentially variation within species, and "trans" is change from one species to another. The authors state their belief that one can "extrapolate" from variation *within* species to evolution *between* species. But they also admit that some of their fellow evolutionists believe that such extrapolation goes beyond all logical limits, like my running a one-minute mile.

What does the evidence suggest? Can evolution from "molecules to man" be extrapolated from selection among dark and light moths? Or are there boundary conditions and logical limits to the amount of change that time, chance, and natural selection can produce?

The answer seems to be: "*Natural selection*, **yes**. *Evolution*, **no**." As it turns out, there are several factors that sharply limit the amount of change that can be produced by time, chance, and Darwinian natural selection. (For exquisite detail on *The Natural Limits to Biological Change*, see Lester and Bohlin.[5])

Perhaps the biggest problem for evolutionists is "the marvelous fit of organisms to their environment." As I mentioned in the first chapter, many adaptations involve whole groups of traits working together, and none of the individual pieces has any survival value ("Darwinian fitness") until the whole set is functioning together. Remember the woodpecker? Let's look at another example.

Since death entered the world, there are many large, predatory fish that roam the oceans. But as they feed on smaller fish and shrimp, their mouths begin to accumulate food debris and parasites. Lacking recourse to a toothbrush, how is such a fish going to clean its teeth?

For several kinds of fish, the answer is a visit to the local cleaning station. These are special areas usually marked by the presence of certain shrimp and small, brightly colored fish, such as wrasses and gobis. Often, fresh from chasing and eating other small fish and shrimp, a predatory fish may swim over to take its place in line (literally!) at the nearest cleaning station. When its turn comes, it opens its mouth wide, baring the vicious-looking teeth.

You might suspect, of course, that such a sight would frighten off the little cleaner fish and shrimp. But no, into the jaws of death swim the little cleaners. Now even a friendly dog will sometimes snap at you if you try to pick off a tick, and it probably irritates the big fish to have a shrimp crawling around on its tongue and little fish picking parasites off the soft tissues of the mouth.(Try to imagine shrimp crawling around on *your* tongue!) But the big fish just hovers there, allowing the cleaners to do their work. It even holds its gill chambers open so that the shrimp can crawl around on the gill filaments picking off parasites!

At the end of all this cleaning, the second "miracle" occurs. You might think the fish would respond, "Ah, clean teeth; SNAP, free meal!" But, no. When the cleaning is done, the big fish lets the little cleaner fish and shrimp back out. Then the big fish swims off—and begins hunting again for little fish and shrimp to eat!

The fantastic relationship just described is called *cleaning symbiosis*. Perhaps you have seen cleaner fish in a major public aquarium, or seen pictures of their behavior in television footage or nature magazines. Cleaning symbiosis is a well-known example of mutualism, an intimate relationship of benefit to both types of species involved, in this case, the "cleaner and the cleanee."

Obviously, cleaning symbiosis has survival value for both types of species involved. But does survival value explain the *origin* of this special relationship? Of course not. It makes sense to talk about survival value only *after* a trait or relationship is already in existence. Question: Did the survival value of this cleaning relationship result from time, chance and struggle, *or* from plan, purpose, and special acts of creation?

The major problem is using Darwinian fitness to explain traits with many interdependent parts when none of the separate parts has *any* survival value. There's certainly no survival value in a small fish swimming into a large fish's mouth on the hope that the big fish has somehow evolved the desire to let it back out! Sea creatures don't provide the only examples of cleaning symbiosis, either. A bird, the Egyptian plover, can walk right into the open mouth of a Nile crocodile—and walk back out again, after cleaning the croc's mouth!

The situation is even more dangerous for the famous "bombardier beetle." The bombardier is an ordinary-looking beetle, but it has an ingenious chemical defense mechanism. Imagine: Here comes a mean ol' beetle-eater, a toad, creeping up behind the seemingly unsuspecting beetle. Just as he gets ready to flash out that long, sticky tongue, the beetle swings its cannon around, and "boom!" It blasts the toad in the face with hot noxious gases at the boiling point of water, and coats the toad's tongue with a foul-tasting residue. Now that doesn't actually kill the toad, but it surely kills its taste for beetles! Pictures show the toad dragging its tongue across the sand trying to get rid of the foul taste.

Successful firing of the bombardier beetle's cannon requires two chemicals (hydrogen peroxide and hydroquinones), enzymes, pressure tanks, and a whole series of nerve and muscle attachments for aim and control. Try to imagine all those parts accumulating by time, chance, and natural selection. One crucial mistake, of course, and "boom!" the would-be bombardier beetle blows *itself* up, and there's surely no evolutionary future in that! Trial and error can lead to improvement only if you survive the error!

Creationists and evolutionists agree that adaptations such as the woodpecker's skull, cleaning symbiosis, and the bombardier beetle's cannon all have survival value. The question is, how did they get that way: by time, chance, and the struggle for survival, or by plan, purpose, and special acts of creation? When it comes to adaptations that require several traits all depending on one another, the more logical inference from the evidence seems to be creation.

Darwin himself was acutely aware of this evidence of creation and the problem it posed for his theory. His chapter in *Origin of Species* on adaptations was *not* titled "Evidence for the Theory" but "Difficulties With the Theory. " In it, he discussed traits that depend on separately meaningless parts. Consider the human eye with the different features required to focus at different distances, to accommodate different amounts of light, and to correct for the "rainbow effect." Regarding the origin of the eye, Darwin wrote these words:

> To suppose that the eye, [with so many parts all working together] . . . could have been formed by natural selection, seems, I freely confess, absurd in the highest degree.

"Absurd in the highest degree." That's Darwin's own opinion of using natural selection to explain the origin of traits that depend on many parts working together.

Modern evolutionists continue to recognize these "difficulties with the theory" of evolution. Harvard's Stephen Gould[6] writes, for example, "What good is half a jaw or half a wing?" Gould also recognizes that many people (especially artists employed by museums and textbook publishers) have tried to present a hypothetical series of gradual changes from one kind to others. So he adds, "These tales, in the 'Just-So Stories' tradition of evolutionary natural history, do not prove anything. . . . Concepts salvaged only by facile speculation do not appeal much to me." Even though Gould is an evolutionist, he recognizes that the classic textbook concept of gradual evolution rests on made-up stories and "facile speculation," and not on facts.

In another article, Gould[7] points out that the perfection of complex structures has always been one of the strongest evidences of creation. After all, he says, "perfection need not have a history," no trial-and-error development over time from chance trait combinations and selection. So, Gould continues, evidence for evolution must be sought in "oddities and imperfections" that clearly show the effects of time and chance.

But creationists recognize imperfection, too. The Bible clearly indicates that "time and chance and struggle" have indeed corrupted what God originally had created in perfection. Imperfection, then, is not the issue; perfection is. And evolutionists from Darwin to Lewontin and Gould admit that

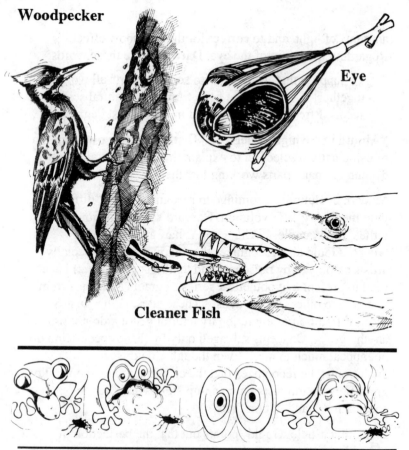

Woodpecker

Eye

Cleaner Fish

Bombardier Beetle

Figure 13-A. Darwin said that, "To suppose the eye . . . could have been formed by natural selection seems, I freely confess, absurd in the highest degree." He included other structures requiring many interdependent parts in a chapter titled "Difficulties With the Theory."

Figure 13-B. Before it can have any survival value, every part of a bombardier beetle's "cannon" must be in place, and the same is true for the woodpecker's set of "drilling tools" and the "nerve wiring" for cleaner-fish behavior. Evolutionist Lewontin says such "perfection of structure was," and I say *is*, "the chief evidence of a Supreme Designer."

"perfection of structure" has always been "the chief evidence of a Supreme Designer."

Darwin's theory also points us back to creative acts when it comes to the origin of traits. In spite of the title of his book, *Origin of Species*, the one thing Darwin never really dealt with was the *origin* of species. That is, he never explained the origin of the truly new traits needed to produce a truly new kind of organism, something *more* than just a variation of some existing kind. There are many other logical limits to extrapolation from natural selection to evolution, but the simplest is this: natural selection cannot explain the *origin* of traits.

Take the famous example of "Darwin's finches" (Fig. 14). On the Galapagos Islands about 600 miles (nearly 1000 km) west of Ecuador, Darwin observed a variety of finches, some with small beaks for catching insects, others with large beaks for crushing seeds, and one with the ability to use spines to pry insects from their tunnels. How did Darwin explain the "origin" of these various finches? Exactly the same way a creationist would. He saw finches with variation in beak type on the South American mainland and presumed these finches might have reached the islands on a vegetation mat or something similar. The ones with seed-crushing beaks survived where seeds were the major food source, and those with insect-catching beaks out-reproduced others where insects were the major source of food. *Given* finches with a variety of beak types, then, natural selection helps us to explain *how* and *where* different varieties *survived* as they multiplied and filled the earth. That, of course, is just what a creationist would say—except, that a Biblical creationist would add that the "struggle and death" part of migration did not begin until man's rebellion ruined the world God had created without death. (Contrast Genesis 1–2 with the Fall in Genesis 3.)

Natural selection works well:it helps us explain how and where traits survive—**if** we have adapted or adaptable traits to start with. In his article on "Adaptation" in the *Scientific American* book *Evolution*, Lewontin[8] emphasizes this point over and over again:

> . . . evolution cannot be described as a process of adaptation because all organisms are already adapted . . .

> . . . adaptation leads to natural selection, natural selection does not necessarily lead to greater adaptation. . . .

That is, adaptation has to come *first*, *before* natural selection can act. Natural selection obviously cannot explain the *origin* of traits or adaptations if the traits have to be there first.

Lewontin recognizes that this simple (but crucial) point is often overlooked, so he gives an example. As a region becomes drier, he says, plants can respond by developing a deeper root system or a thicker cuticle (waxy coating) on the leaves, but "*only if* their gene pool contains genetic variation for root length or cuticle thickness." (Emphasis added.) Here again, the genes for deep roots and thick, waxy coats must be present among the genes of a kind *before* natural selection can select them. And if the genes are already there, we are talking only about variation within kind: i.e., creation, not evolution. As creationists were saying *even before* Darwin's time, natural selection does *not* explain the *origin* of species or traits, but only their *preservation*.

Lewontin is an evolutionist and outspoken anti-creationist, but he honestly recognizes the same limitations of natural selection that creation scientists do:

> . . . natural selection operates essentially to enable the organisms to *maintain* their state of adaptation rather than to improve it. (Emphasis added.)

Natural selection does not lead to continual improvement (evolution); it only helps to maintain features that organisms

Figure 14. "Darwin's Finches." Darwin explained the location of finches with different beak types on the Galapagos Islands the same way a creationist would, by starting with a population of finches with variation in beak type. In fact, the creationist Edward Blyth published the concept of natural selection 24 years before Darwin did, and he used it to help explain how created kinds spread throughout different environments after sin brought struggle and death to the earth.

already have (creation). Lewontin also notes that extinct species seem to have been just as fit to survive as modern ones, so he adds:

> . . . natural selection over the long run does *not* seem to improve a species' chances of survival, but simply enables it to 'track,' or *keep up with*, the constantly changing environment. (Emphasis added.)

It seems to me that natural selection works only because each kind was created with sufficient variety to multiply and fill the earth in all its ecologic and geographic variety. Without realizing it at the time, Darwin actually discovered important evidence pointing both to God's *creation* (the variation) and to the *corruption* of creation (struggle and death).

Pangenesis: Use and Disuse

Darwin called natural selection "the preservation of favored races," and he recognized that selection alone could not explain origin. When it came to the actual origin of new traits, Darwin wrote that it was "from use and disuse, from the direct and indirect actions of the environment" that new traits arose. About 40 years before Darwin, a famous French evolutionist, Jean Lamarck, argued for this kind of evolution based on the *inheritance of traits acquired by use and disuse*. Most books on the subject hint that we should laugh at Lamarck—but Darwin believed exactly the same thing.

Consider the supposed origin of the giraffe. According to both Darwin and Lamarck, the story begins back on the African prairies a long time ago. Because of prolonged drought, the prairie dried up. But there were green leaves up in the trees, and some of the animals started stretching their necks to reach them. As a result, their necks got a little longer (Fig. 15). Now that could be partly true. If you really work at it hard enough and long enough, you could add a little bit to your height. People used to do that to get into the army or some special service where you have to be a certain height. The problem,

Figure 15. For the *origin* of new traits, Darwin (like Lamarck) resorted to "use and disuse" and the inheritance of acquired characteristics. Giraffes got longer necks, for example, because their ancestors stretched for leaves in trees, then passed on more neck "pangenes" to their offspring. This idea of "progress through effort" contributed to the early popularity of evolution, but has since been disproved.

however, is that the offspring of "stretched" parents start off just as small as all the others. The long neck could not be passed on to the next generation.

Like others of his time, Darwin didn't know about the mechanism of heredity. He thought that at reproduction each organ produced "*pangenes*" that would collect in the blood and flow to the reproductive organs. So, a bigger neck made more neck pangenes. Some people still believe this sort of concept. You've probably run into people who say, for instance, that people will eventually have bigger heads because we think a lot, and no toes because we wear shoes all the time. Darwin even used pangenes to "explain" why (in his opinion) wives grew to resemble their husbands as both got older.

Science has since disproved these "flimsy facts" of early evolutionary thought, but back in Darwin's time, pangenes captured people's imagination probably even more than natural selection did. To some, Darwin's original theory of evolution suggested continual progress. How do you make something happen? By use and disuse. If you want to get smarter, use your brain, and both you and your children will be smarter. If you want to be strong, use your muscles, and not only will you get stronger, but so will your children.

Well, almost unfortunately, that's not the modern theory of evolution. The use-disuse theory didn't work and had to be discarded. A man named Weismann, for example, cut off the tails of mice for twenty-some generations, only to find that baby mice were still born with tails. Traits acquired by use and disuse just don't affect heredity.

Mutations

The modern evolutionist is called a *neo*-Darwinian. He still accepts Darwin's ideas about natural selection, but something new (neo-) has been added. The modern evolutionist believes that new traits come about by chance, by random changes in genes called "mutations," and *not* by use and disuse.

Almost everyone has heard about mutations—from Saturday morning cartoons or horror movies, if nowhere else. In those flicks, some atomic disaster produces people with gnarled skin, one big bulging eye, and other "new traits." In the real world, mutations are responsible for a number of genetic defects, including hemophilia (bleeders' disease), loss of protective color in the skin and eyes (albinism), and certain kinds of cancer and brain malfunction.

We have abundant evidence that various kinds of radiations, errors in DNA replication, and certain chemicals can indeed produce mutations, and mutations in reproductive cells can be passed on to future generations. Fig. 16 shows some of the changes that have been brought about in fruit-fly wings because of mutations: shorter wings, very short wings, curled wings, spread-apart wings, miniature wings, wings without cross veins. Students in my genetics classes work with these fruit flies each year, crossing different ones and working out inheritance patterns.

Then there's the flu virus. Why haven't we yet been able to solve the flu problem? Part of the problem is that this year's vaccine and your own antibodies are only good against last year's flu. (They don't usually tell you that when you get the shot, but it's already out of date.) The smallpox virus has the common decency to stay the same year in and year out, so once you're vaccinated or build up an immunity, that's it. But the flu virus mutates quite easily, so each year its proteins are slightly different from last year's. They are still flu viruses, but they don't quite fit our antibodies, so we have to build up our immunity all over again. When it recombines with animal viruses (on the average of once every ten years), the problem is even worse.

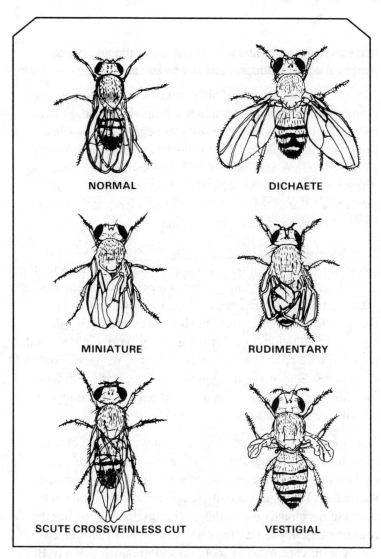

Figure 16. Mutations are random changes in genes (DNA), often caused by radiation. The mutations in the wings above were produced by X-raying fruit flies. According to the modern, *neo-Darwinian* view, mutations are the source of new traits for evolution, and selection culls out the fittest combinations (or eliminates the "unfittest") that are first produced just by chance. Mutations certainly occur, but are there limits to extrapolating from mutational changes to evolutionary changes (e.g., "fish to philosopher")?

Mutations are certainly real. They have profound effects on our lives. And, according to the neo-Darwinian evolutionists, mutations are the raw material for evolution.

But is that possible? Can mutations produce real evolutionary changes? Don't make any mistakes here. Mutations are real; they're something we observe; they do make changes in traits. But the question remains: do they produce *evolutionary* changes? Do they really produce *new* traits? Do they really help to explain that postulated change from molecules to man, or fish to philosopher?

The answer seems to be: "*Mutations*, **yes**. *Evolution,* **no**." In the last analysis, mutations really don't help evolutionary theory at all. There are three major problems or limits (and many minor ones) that prevent scientific extrapolation from mutational change to evolutionary change.

(1) *Mathematical challenges*. Problem number one is the mathematical. I won't dwell on this one, because it's written up in many books and widely acknowledged by evolutionists themselves as a serious problem for their theory.

Fortunately, mutations are very rare. They occur on an average of perhaps once in every ten million duplications of a DNA molecule (10^7, a one followed by seven zeroes). That's fairly rare. On the other hand, it's not *that* rare. Our bodies contain nearly 100 trillion cells (10^{14}). So the odds are quite good that we have a couple of cells with a mutated form of almost any gene. A test tube can hold millions of bacteria, so, again, the odds are quite good that there will be mutant forms among them.

The mathematical problem for evolution comes when you want a *series* of r*elated* mutations. The odds of getting two mutations that are related to one another is the product of the separate probabilities: one in 10^7 x 10^7, or 10^{14}. That's a one followed by 14 zeroes, a hundred trillion! Any two mutations might produce no more than a fly with a wavy edge on a bent wing. That's a long way from producing a truly new structure, and certainly a long way from changing a fly into some new kind of organism. You need more mutations for that. So, what are the odds of getting *three* mutations in a row? That's one in a billion trillion (10^{21}). Suddenly, the ocean isn't big enough to hold enough bacteria to make it likely for you to find a bacterium with three simultaneous or sequential related mutations.

What about trying for *four* related mutations? One in 10^{28}. Suddenly, the earth isn't big enough to hold enough organisms to make that very likely. And we're talking about only four mutations. It would take many more than that to change a fish into a philosopher, or even a fish into a frog. Four mutations don't even make a start toward any real evolution. But already at this point some evolutionists have given up the classic idea of evolution, because it just plainly doesn't work.

It was at this level (just four related mutations) that microbiologists gave up on the idea that mutations could explain why some bacteria are resistant to four different antibiotics at the same time. The odds against the mutation explanation were simply too great, so they began to look for another mechanism—and they found it. First of all, using cultures that are routinely kept for long periods of time, they found out that bacteria were resistant to antibiotics, even *before* commercial antibiotics were "invented." Genetic variability was "built right into" the bacteria. Did the nonresistant varieties get resistant by mutation? No. Resistant forms were already present. Furthermore, certain bacteria have little rings of DNA, called plasmids, that they trade around among themselves, and they passed on their resistance to antibiotics in that way. It wasn't mutation and asexual reproduction at all, just ordinary recombination and variation within kind.

Bacteria *can* be made antibiotic resistant by mutation, but biologist Novick[9] calls such forms "evolutionary cripples."

The mutation typically damages a growth factor, so that the mutationally crippled bacteria can scarcely survive outside the lab. The antibiotic resistance carried by plasmids results from enzymes produced to break down the antibiotic. Such bacteria do not have their growth crippled by mutation. Their resistance is by design.

But why, you might well ask, would God create antibiotic resistance? It's possible God designed antibiotic resistance in bacteria, and antibiotic production by fungi, to balance the growth of these prolific organisms in the soil. Only after the corruption of creation did some bacteria become disease causers, making antibiotic resistance "inadvertently" a medical problem.

Contrary to popular opinion, drug resistance in bacteria does *not* demonstrate evolution. It doesn't even demonstrate the production of favorable mutations. It *does* demonstrate natural selection (or a sort of artificial selection, in this case), but only selection among already existing variations within a kind. It also demonstrates that when the odds that a particular process will produce a given effect get too low, good scientists normally look for a better explanation, such as the plasmid explanation for resistance to multiple antibiotics.

At this point, evolutionists often say that "Time is the hero of the plot." That's what I used to say to my students. "Sure, the odds are low, but there's all that time, nearly 5 billion years!" But 5 billion years is only about 10^{17} seconds, and the whole universe contains fewer than 10^{80} atoms. So even by the wildest "guesstimates," the universe isn't old enough or big enough to reach odds like the 1 in $10^{3,000,000}$ that Huxley, an evolutionist, estimated as the odds against the evolution of the horse.

Way back in 1967, a prestigious group of internationally known biologists and mathematicians gathered at the Wistar Institute to consider *Mathematical Challenges to the*

Neo-Darwinian Interpretation of Evolution.[10] All present were evolutionists, and they agreed, as the preface clearly states, that no one would be questioning evolution itself. The only question was, could mutations serve as the basis—with natural selection—as a mechanism for evolutionary change? The answer of the mathematicians: No. Just plain *no*!

Emotions ran high. After a particularly telling paper by Marcel Shutzenberger of the University of Paris, the chairman of the gathering. C. H. Waddington, said, "Your argument is simply that life must have come about by special creation!" The stenographer records, "Schutzenberger: No! Voices: No!" Anything but creation; it wasn't even fair (in spite of the evidence!) to bring up the word.

Dr. Waddington later called himself, impressively, a "post-neo-Darwinist," someone who believes in evolution, but who also believes that mutation-selection cannot explain how evolution can occur. Many research evolutionists (but not many textbook writers or teachers) recognize the need for a new generation of evolutionists to forge the "post-neo-Darwinian synthesis."

In his chapter "Beyond the Reach of Chance," Denton[11] discusses attempts to simulate evolutionary processes on computers. He concludes with these strong words:

> If complex computer programs cannot be changed by random mechanisms, then surely the same must apply to the genetic programs of living organisms. *The fact that systems in every way analogous to living organisms cannot undergo evolution by pure trial and error* [i.e., by mutation and selection] and that their functional distribution invariably conforms to an improbable discontinuum *comes, in my opinion, very close to a formal disproof of the whole Darwinian paradigm of nature.* By what strange capacity do living organisms *defy the laws of*

chance which are apparently obeyed by all analogous complex systems? (Emphasis added).

Most gratifyingly, Denton seems to look beyond the merely negative insufficiency of chance to glimpse a solution to "The Puzzle of Perfection," as he calls it, in the "design hypothesis:"

> It is the sheer universality of perfection, the fact that everywhere we look, we find an elegance and ingenuity of an absolutely transcending quality, which so mitigates against the idea of chance. . . . In practically every field of fundamental biological research ever-increasing levels of design and complexity are being revealed at an ever-accelerating rate. The credibility of natural selection is weakened, therefore, not only by the perfection we have already glimpsed but by the expectation of further as yet undreampt [*sic*] of depths of ingenuity and complexity (p. 342).

Unfortunately, we also have evidence that the transcendent ingenuity and design Denton sees has been marred and scarred. In that sense, mathematics isn't even the most serious challenge to using mutations as the basis for evolution.

(2) *Upward or downward*? Even more serious is the fact that mutations are "going the wrong way" as far as evolution is concerned. Almost every mutation we know is identified by the disease or abnormality that it causes. Creationists use *mutations* to explain the *origin of parasites and disease*, the *origin of hereditary defects*, and the *loss of traits*. In other words, time, chance, and random changes do just what we normally expect: tear things down and make matters worse. Using mutations to explain the *breakdown* of existing genetic order (creation-corruption) is quite the opposite of using mutations to explain the *build up* of genetic order (evolution). Clearly, creation-corruption is the most direct inference from the effects of mutations that scientists actually observe.

By producing defects or blocking the normal function of certain genes, mutations have introduced numerous genetic abnormalities into the human population. The hemophilia (bleeders' disease) that afflicted the royal houses of Europe may have arisen as a mutant of a clotting-factor gene in Queen Victoria, for example; and the dread Tay-Sach's Disease may have arisen in Czechoslovakia in the 1920's as a mutation in the gene for producing an enzyme crucial to brain function.

Some people like to call mutations "the means of creation." But mutations don't create; they corrupt! Both logically and often observationally, as in the examples above, the ordered state must come before mutations can disorder it. Mutations are real, all right, but they point to a *corruption* of the created order by time and chance.

As a matter of fact, human beings are now subject to over 3500 mutational disorders. Fortunately, we don't show as many defects as we carry. The reason they don't show up is that we each have two sets of genes, one set of genes from our mothers and another set from our fathers. The "bad genes" we inherit from our mothers' side are usually covered up by our fathers' genes, and vice versa. We can see what is likely to happen when an animal is born with only one set of genes. Fig. 17, based on a description in a genetics textbook, represents the rare case of a turkey that was hatched from an unfertilized egg, so it had just one set of chromosomes. The poor bird couldn't hold its head up; instead, it bobbed up and down from a neurological disorder. The feathers were missing in patches, and it finally had to be transferred to a germ-free chamber because its resistance to disease was so low.

Now here's the basis for a good horror story. Picture a mirror at the end of a dark hall. You claw your way through the spider webs to reach the mirror, and then you press a button. The mirror then splits you in two halves, so you can see what you would look like if you had only your mother's genes or

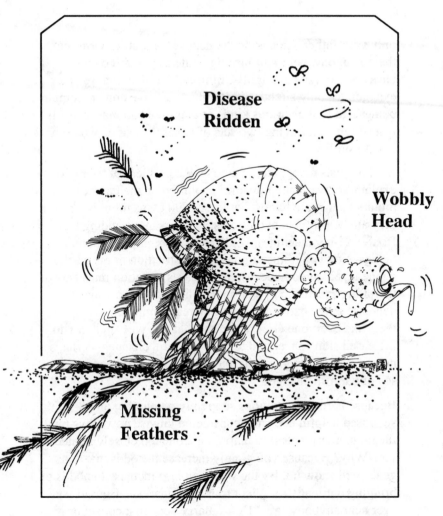

Disease Ridden

Wobbly Head

Missing Feathers

Figure 17. Mutations are mostly harmful, and, as time goes on, they impose an increasingly heavy *"genetic burden"* on a species. The turkey above, lacking a second set of genes to mask its hereditary defects, could scarcely survive. Creationists use mutations to help explain the origin of parasites and disease. Some evolutionists still believe that time, chance, and occasional favorable mutations provide the raw material for "upward-onward" progress, but the "post-neo-Darwinists" are looking for other means to explain evolution.

only your father's genes. In the next scene, you're writhing there in agony, your hair turning white as you fall over backward and die of fright! Unfortunately, that picture exaggerates only slightly what mutations have done to human beings and to the various kinds of plants and animals as well. If it weren't for having two sets of genes, few of us would be able to survive.

Evolutionists recognize, of course, the problem of trying to explain "onward and upward" evolution on the basis of mutations that are harmful at least 1000 times more often than they are helpful. No evolutionist believes that standing in front of X-ray machines would eventually improve human beings. No evolutionist argues that destruction of the earth's ozone layer is good because it increases mutation rates and, therefore, speeds up evolution. Evolutionists know that decrease in the ozone layer will increase mutation rates, but they, like everyone else, recognize that this will lead only to increased skin cancer and to other harmful changes. Perhaps a helpful change *might* occur, but it would be drowned in the sea of harmful changes.

Because harmful mutations so greatly outnumber any supposed helpful ones, it's considered unwise nowadays (and illegal in many states) to marry someone too closely related to you. Why? Because you greatly increase the odds that bad genes will show up. By the way, you also increase the odds of bringing out really excellent trait combinations. But did you ever hear anybody say, "Don't marry your first cousin or you'll have a genius for a child?" They don't usually say that, because the odds of something bad happening are far, far, far, far, far greater.

That would not have been a problem, by the way, shortly after creation (no problem for Cain and his wife, for example). Until mutations had a chance to accumulate in the human population, no such risk of bad combinations existed. Mutations are often carried as "hidden genes" (recessives) that are difficult to eliminate by selection, so they tend to build up in populations. The build-up of mutations with time poses a serious problem for plants and animals, as well as for human beings, and time, evolution's "hero," only *worsens* the problem of mutational decay.

Geneticists, even evolutionary geneticists, refer to the problem as *"genetic load"* or *"genetic burden."* In their textbook on evolution, Dobzhansky et al.[12] state clearly that the term is meant to imply a burden that "weighs down" a species and lowers its genetic quality. In an article paradoxically titled "The Mechanisms of Evolution," Francisco Ayala[13] defines a mutation as "an error" in DNA. Then he explains that inbreeding has revealed that mutations in fruit flies have produced "extremely short wings, deformed bristles, blindness, and other serious defects." Does that sound like "the raw material for evolution?"

It's not that beneficial mutations are theoretically impossible. Bacteria that lose the ability to digest certain sugars, for example, can regain that ability by mutation. That's no help to evolution, however, since the bacterium only gets back to where it started, but at least the mutant is helpful.

Actually, only three evolutionists have ever given me an example of a beneficial mutation. It was the same example all three times: *sickle-cell anemia*. Sickle-cell anemia is a disease of red blood cells. Why would anyone call that a beneficial mutation? Well, in certain parts of Africa, the death rate from malaria is quite high. Malaria is caused by a tiny, one-celled organism that gets inside the red blood cells and eats up the hemoglobin. Now, that particular germ doesn't like sickle-cell hemoglobin. Carriers of one sickle-cell gene produce about half normal and half sickle-cell hemoglobin, and the malaria germ leaves them alone, too. So, carriers don't get malaria. But the cost is high: 25% of the children of carriers can die of sickle-cell anemia, and another 25% are subject to malaria. If you want to call that a good mutation, you're welcome to it! It seems doubtful to me that real improvement of human beings would result from accumulating that kind of "beneficial" mutant, and certainly hemoglobin's ability to carry oxygen was not improved.

The gene for sickle-cell anemia has built up to high levels in certain African populations, not because it is "beneficial" in some abstract sense, but simply because the death rate from anemia in those areas is less than the death rate from malaria. Natural selection is a "blind" process that automatically accumulates genes for short-term survival, even if it reduces the long-term survival of the species. For that reason, evolutionists recognize that natural selection can occasionally lead to "mischievous results" detrimental to genetic quality. That's the effect I think we're seeing with sickle-cell anemia (Fig. 18).

Furthermore, when the frequency of the sickle-cell gene reaches 18%, natural selection for it "stops." That's the point at which the death rates from sickle-cell anemia and malaria balance, demonstrating conclusively that sickle-cell anemia is **not** a suitable model for the continuous genetic expansion that evolutionists seek.

Suppose I told you I had found a way to make cars run uphill without using gasoline. Then, as you watched in eager anticipation, I showed you how applying the brakes would make the car run downhill more slowly. Would you believe I had discovered a means for getting cars to run uphill without fuel? Similarly, natural selection can and does slow the rate of genetic decay produced by accumulating mutations (as it does with sickle-cell hemoglobin), but that hardly proves that mutation-selection produces upward and onward progress!

A better example of favorable mutation might be the one possibly involved in the change from teosinte into corn, as described by Nobel laureate George Beadle.[14] But as Beadle points out, the mutation was favorable to people, not to corn.

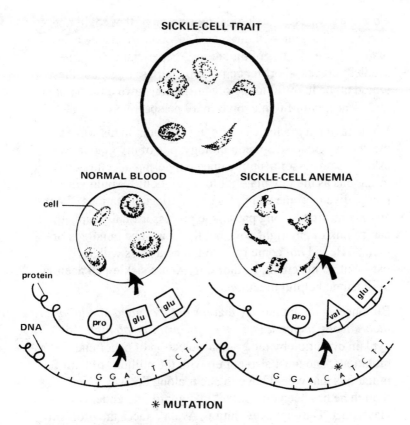

SICKLE-CELL TRAIT

NORMAL BLOOD

SICKLE-CELL ANEMIA

cell

protein

DNA

G G A C T T C T T

G G A C A T C T T

✳ MUTATION

Figure 18. "Sickle-cell anemia" is often given as an example of a favorable mutation, because people carrying sickle-cell hemoglobin in their red blood cells (Ss) are resistant to malaria. But the price for this protection is high: 25% of the children of carriers may die of the anemia (ss), and another 25% (SS) are subject to malaria. The gene will automatically be selected where the death rate from malaria is high, but evolutionists themselves admit that short-term advantages—all that natural selection can ever favor—can produce "mischievous results" detrimental to long-term survival. What do you think? Is sickle-cell anemia a "mischievous result," or a good example of evolutionary progress? (Drawing after Parker, Reynolds, and Reynolds.*Heredity*. 2nd ed. Chicago: Educational Methods, Inc., 1977.)

Corn, he says, is a "biological monstrosity" that could not survive on its own, without man's special care. There are many other examples of mutations "beneficial" to people: seedless grapes, short-legged sheep, hairless dogs, but these would all be harmful to the organism in its own environment and, hence, harmful in evolutionary perspective.

While taking a graduate course in evolution on his way to a master-of-science degree in biology, one of my graduates asked his professor a simple question during a lecture on mutations as the raw material for evolution: "Would you please give us some examples of beneficial mutations?" After an uncomfortably long pause, the professor finally replied, "I can't think of any right now, but there must be hundreds of them." He did *not* come back to the next class with a list—but, to his credit, he didn't try to use sickle-cell anemia to illustrate helpful mutations.

But once again, let me say that *it's not that good mutations are theoretically impossible. Rather, the price is too high.* To explain evolution by the gradual selection of beneficial mutations, one must also put up with the millions of harmful mutations that would have to occur along the way. Even though he has been one of the "old guard" defenders of classic neo-Darwinian evolution, Ayala[15] faces the problem squarely in his article in the *Scientific American* book *Evolution*. He is talking about variation within species (not kind, but species, the smallest possible unit). He says that variation within species is much greater than Darwin postulated. He speaks of such variation as "enormous" and "staggering." Yet when he gets to the actual figures, the variation is less than I, as a creationist, would have expected. (Ayala did say his figures *under*estimated the real variation.)

For creationists, all this variation poses no problem at all. If living things were created to multiply and fill the earth, then great variation within kind is simply good design. There would be no price to pay for created variability, since it would result from creation, *not* from time, chance, and mutation. (Mutations have introduced further variability since creation was corrupted, but it's the kind of variability a bull introduces into a china shop!)

What problem did Ayala, as an evolutionist, see with all this staggering variability? Just this: For each beneficial mutant a species accumulated, the price would be a thousand or more harmful mutations. When genetic burden gets too great, offspring are so likely to have serious hereditary defects that the ability of the species to survive is threatened.

Time only makes this evolutionary problem worse. Thanks to our accumulated genetic burden, serious hereditary defects are present in perhaps 5% of all human births, and that percentage greatly increases among the children of closely related parents. All of us have some genetic shortcomings, and it's really only by common consent that most of us agree to call each other "normal."

Natural selection cannot save us from this awful situation either. Selection can and does eliminate or reduce the worst mutations—but only when these mutants come to visible (phenotypic) expression. Most mutations "hide" as recessives, "invisible" to selection, and continue to build up in secret at multiple loci, somewhat like a *"genetic cancer"* slowly but steadily eating away at genetic quality.

If early evolutionists had known what we know now about mutations, it's most unlikely that mutations would ever have been proposed as the pathway to evolutionary progress.

(3) *Mutations point back to creation.* Mathematics and genetic load are huge problems for evolution, but the biggest reason mutations cannot lead to evolution is an extremely simple one. It's so simple, I'm almost afraid to say it. But really, *mutations presuppose creation.* After all, *mutations are only changes in genes that already exist.*

Most mutations are caused by radiation or replication errors. But what do you have to have before you can have a mutation? Obviously, the gene has to be there first, before the radiation can hit it or before it can make a copying mistake. In one sense, it's as simple as that: the gene has to be there *before* it can mutate. All you get as a result of mutation is just a varied form of an already-existing gene, i.e., variation within kind. (Fig. 19.)

Genes of the same kind, like those for straight and curly hair or those for yellow and green seeds, are called alleles. There are over 300 alleles of the hemoglobin gene. That's a lot of variation, but all those alleles produce hemoglobin, a protein for carrying oxygen in red blood cells (none better than the normal allele). By concept and definition, alleles are just variants of a given gene, producing variation in a given trait. Mutations produce only alleles, which means they can produce only variation *within kind* (creation), *not* change from one kind to others (evolution).

To make evolution happen—or even to make evolution a scientific theory—evolutionists need some kind of "genetic script writer" to increase the quantity and quality of genetic information. Mutations are just "typographic errors" that occur as genetic script is copied. Mutations have no ability to compose genetic sentences, and thus no ability to make evolution happen at all.

By What Means?

Once in a while an evolutionist will say that any farmer who practices selective breeding is practicing evolution. But as one farmer put it, "Mister, when I cross pigs, I get pigs. I don't get dogs and cats and horses." If the point is that obvious, then even scientists who believe in evolution ought to see it. And they do.

Harvard's Stephen Gould[16] quite clearly recognizes the difference between evolution and mutations. Evolution, he

Abrupt Appearance: Stasis

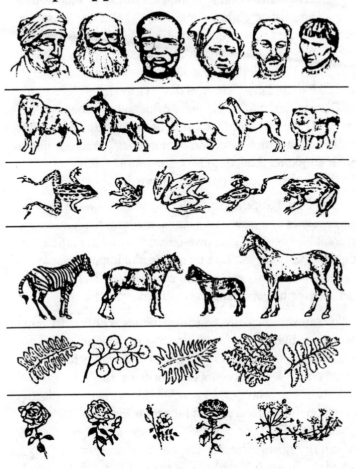

Figure 19. The most logical inference from our scientific observations of mutation, selection, and genetic recombination would seem to be *variation within created kinds*. There's no "genetic burden" to bear if variety is produced by creation instead of time, chance, and mutation. But could there be enough variation in each created kind to produce all the diversity we see today? Creationists now have some promising answers to that question. (Drawing after Bliss. *Origins Two Models.* 2nd ed. Colorado Springs: Master Books. 1978.

says, involves "profound structural transitions," such as a change from fish to philosopher (*macro*evolution). Mutations, he says, produce only minor variations, like those we see in experiments with "flies in bottles" that start as flies and end up as flies. Then Gould chides his fellow evolutionists for illogical extrapolation. He says that "Orthodox neo-Darwinians extrapolate these even and continuous changes to the most profound structural transitions. . . ." For the old line mutation-selection evolutionist, "macroevolution (major structural transition) is nothing more than microevolution (flies in bottles) extended."

But then Gould asks himself, "How can such processes change a gnat or a rhinoceros into something fundamentally different?" Answering his own question in a later article, Gould[17] simply says: "That theory [orthodox neo-Darwinian extrapolationalism], as a general proposition, is effectively dead, despite its persistence as textbook orthodoxy."

Gould believes our knowledge of genetics is now sufficient to reject the explanation of evolution as the slow, gradual selection of small mutational changes. He prefers to believe instead that evolution occurs in giant steps, radical restructuring of whole DNA sets, producing what he himself calls "hopeful monsters." But he admits that no such hopeful monster has ever been observed. His new theory, then, is not any sort of logical inference from observations, but a fantastic faith in the future of a theory that the facts have failed.

And Gould is far from an isolated example. Back in October of 1980, the world's leading evolutionists met in Chicago for a conference summarized popularly by Adler and Carey in *Newsweek*[18] and professionally by Lewin in *Science*.[19] According to the professional summary,

> The central question of the Chicago conference was whether the mechanisms underlying microevolution can

be extrapolated to explain the phenomena of macro-evolution.

That is, the processes of mutation, selection, and sexual recombination all produce variation within kind (microevolution—or creationist adaptation), but can these processes be logically extended (extrapolated) to explain the presumed evolutionary change generally from simpler to more complex types (macroevolution)?

At the risk of doing violence to the positions of some of the people at the meeting, the answer can be given as a clear, No.

Just plain *No*! One cannot logically extrapolate from mutation-selection to evolution. Creationists pointed out a series of logical and observational limits to that gross over-extrapolation decades ago, and we are pleased, of course, that the world's leading evolutionists now agree with us—without giving us any credit—that the textbook and television pictures of minuscule mutations being slowly selected to produce elaborate evolution are just flatly, false.

At this point, many evolutionists say, in effect, "Well, at least we agree that evolution is a fact, even though we are not certain about the mechanism." Although I used to say that myself, it now sounds almost comically incongruous, both to me and to Colin Patterson,[20] leading paleontologist at the British Museum. Evolutionists used to accuse creationists of affirming the fact of diversity without offering any mechanism to explain it, says Patterson, but now, he says, that is what evolutionists are doing. A theory that simply accepts the diversity of life without offering a mechanism to explain *how* that diversity came into being, adds Patterson, cannot be considered a scientific theory at all!

Evolutionists ultimately believe, to use an example from secular television,[21] that frogs turn into princes. But if the mechanism turned out to be the kiss of a princess, rather than time, chance, and the properties of matter, then the evolutionary explanation for change would be wrong, and the theory falsified in this instance. Whether it's the changing of frogs into princes, fish into philosophers, or molecules into man, calling evolution a fact without at least broadly specifying a mechanism is both non-science and non-sense—unless evolutionists are willing to consider the kiss of a princess a potentially valid evolutionary hypothesis!

Creationists don't believe that frogs turn into princes at all, of course, but, rather, that frogs and people were separately created from the same kinds of molecular "building blocks." Remember the tumbled pebble and the arrowhead (Fig. 1)? Both were shaped from the same substance, one by the mechanism of time and chance acting on the inherent properties of matter, the other by the mechanism of plan and purpose, producing properties of organization. Mechanism—the explanation of *how*—is, therefore, the heart of the creation-evolution issue. Substance, adaptations, and change are the "givens" or "facts" *shared* by those on both sides. The central question is: *How*—by what means or mechanism—did these patterns of order come into being, by time and chance like the tumbled pebble, or, like the arrowhead, by plan and purpose?

The large majority of evolutionists at the Chicago conference agreed that the neo-Darwinian mechanism of mutation-selection could no longer be regarded as a scientifically tenable explanation for the origin and diversity of living things. Unfortunately, many of the evolutionists, some quite reluctantly, seemed willing to put their hope, instead, in the "hopeful monster" mechanism resurrected by Gould and others. A few were willing to fight what *Newsweek* called a "rear guard action" on behalf of otherwise-defunct neo-Darwinism. But some scientists are willing to look for truly new hypotheses that have the promise of stimulating more fruitful research.

One such scientist is Pierre Grasse'. He has been called "the dean of French zoologists," yet he rejects mutation-selection as a means of evolutionary change[22] in scathing words. Mutations are "merely hereditary fluctuations around a median position; a swing to the right, a swing to the left, but no final evolutionary effect." He goes on to say that mutations "are not complementary. . . , nor are they cumulative." That is, they don't work together, and they don't add up to anything. "They modify what pre-exists," says Grasse', which means you can get no more from mutations than variation within kind. In fact, you get even *less*, because mutations are mostly harmful, says Grasse', producing "downhill" changes, not "upward-onward" evolution. He strongly condemns attempts to use selection to salvage a few favorable mutations for evolution:

> Directed by all-powerful selection, chance becomes a sort of providence [i.e., "God"]. . . which is secretly worshipped.

Grasse' is not (yet) a creationist. But he does say that his knowledge of the living world convinces him that there must be some "internal force" involved in the history of life. That may remind you of Albert Szent-Gyorgyi, the Nobel-prize winner, who said that the origin of complex traits by random mutation has the probability of *zero*. In the first chapter, I mentioned that his observations of living things forced Szent-Gyorgyi, like Grasse', to postulate at least a *creative force*.

Maybe you also remember Garrett Hardin from the first chapter. Because of "nature's challenges to evolutionary theory," he asked, "Is the [evolutionary] framework wrong? Was Paley right?" That is, can we infer creation from the kind of design we see among living things? "Think about it."

That's why it's so vital that our students be given every opportunity to explore all aspects of the origins' issue, including *all* the scientific data. (In my experience, by the way, Canadian and Australian students have much greater academic freedom in this area than students in America, the so-called "land of the free.") After all, it is only those students who have access to *all* the relevant information on a topic who are truly free to "think about it."

Variation Within Created Kinds

But, "think about it!" doesn't mean "Stop here!" It means "Start here!"

I have been saying, perhaps too often, that the weight of evidence points to "variation within the created kinds." Do I really mean that all the tremendous variety we see today was built right into the created kinds—just a pair as a minimum for most kinds and perhaps a dozen in one-celled forms with multiple sexes? Could there be enough variation in two created human beings, for example, to produce all the variation among human beings we see today?

Answer: "Yes, indeed; no problem!" I get some help here from an unexpected source, evolutionist Francisco Ayala.[23] He says that human beings are "heterozygous" for 6.7% of their genes on the average. That means that 6 or 7 times in a 100, the pair of genes for a given trait differ, like the genes for free or attached ear lobes, or for rolling or not rolling the tongue. Now this may not seem like much. But Ayala calculates a single human couple with just "6.7% variety" could produce 10^{2017} children (mathematically, not physically!) before they would run out of variation and have to produce an identical twin. That's a 1 followed by 2,017 zeroes! The number of atoms in the known universe is a mere 10^{80}, nothing at all compared with the variety that is present in the genes of just two human beings!

Take human skin color, for example. First of all, it may surprise you to learn that all of us (except albinos) have exactly the *same* skin-coloring agent. It's a protein called melanin. We all have the same basic skin color, just different amounts of it. (Not a very big difference, is it?) How long would it take to get all the variation in the amount of skin color we see among people today? A million years? No. A thousand years? No. Answer: *just one generation!*

Let's see how that works. The amount of skin color we have depends on at least two pairs of genes. Let's call these genes **A** and **B**. People with the darkest skin color have genes **AABB** as their genotype (set of genes for a trait); those with very light skins have **aabb.** People with two "capital-letter" genes would be "medium-skinned," and those with one or three such genes would be a shade lighter or a shade darker.

Suppose we start with two medium-skinned parents, **AaBb**. Fig. 20 is a genetic square that shows the kind of children they could have. Less than half (only 6 of the 16 combinations) would be medium-skinned like their parents. Four each would be a shade darker or lighter. One in 16 of the children of medium-skinned parents (**AaBb**) would have the darkest possible skin color (**AABB**), while the chances are also 1 in 16 that a brother or sister will have the very lightest skin color (**aabb**). (For details, see Parker, Reynolds, and Reynolds.[24])

The Bible doesn't tell us what skin color our first parents had, but, from a design point of view, the "middle" makes a great beginning. Starting with medium-skinned parents (**AaBb**), it would take only one generation to produce all the variation we see in human skin color today. In fact, this is the normal situation in India today. Some Indians are as dark as the darkest Africans, and some—perhaps a brother or sister in the same family—as light as the lightest Europeans. I once knew a family from India that included members with every major skin color you could see anywhere in the world.

But now notice what happens if human groups were isolated after creation. If those with very dark skins (**AABB**) migrate into the same areas and/or marry only those with very dark

Maximum Variation
AaBa x AaBa

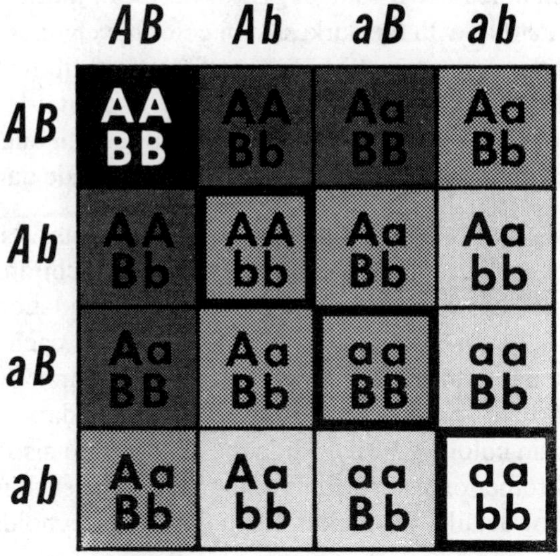

	AB	*Ab*	*aB*	*ab*
AB	AA BB	AA Bb	Aa BB	Aa Bb
Ab	AA Bb	AA bb	Aa Bb	Aa bb
aB	Aa BB	Aa Bb	aa BB	aa Bb
ab	Aa Bb	Aa bb	aa Bb	aa bb

Only
Dark
AABB

Only
Medium
aaBB

Only
Light
aabb

Figure 20. All human beings have *the same* basic skin-color agent (melanin), just different amounts of it. From parents created with medium skin color as diagrammed, all the variation we see today could be produced in just *one generation*. In the same way, plants and animals created with a mixture of genes could have filled all of the earth's ecologic and geographic variety. As people break up into groups, however, some groups would develop limited variability—only dark, only medium, or only light as indicated.

skins, then all their children will have very dark skins. (**AABB** is the only possible combination of **AB** egg and sperm cells, which are the only types that can be produced by **AABB** parents.) Similarly, parents with very light skins (**aabb**) can have only very light-skinned children, since they don't have any **A** or **B** genes to pass on. Even certain medium-skinned parents (**AAbb or aaBB**) can get "locked-in" to having only medium-skinned children, like the Orientals, Polynesians, and some of my ancestors, the Native Americans.

Where people with different skin colors get together again (as they do in the West Indies, for example), you find the full range of variation again—nothing less, but nothing more either, than what we started with. Clearly, all this is *variation within kind*.

"Gene pool" refers to all the different genes that are present in a population. There are at least four skin-color genes in the human gene pool: **A**, **a**, **B**, **b**. That total human gene pool for skin color can be found in just one person with medium skin color (**AaBb**), or it can be "spread around" among many people with visibly different skin colors. In fact, the gene frequencies (percents of each gene) in one **AaBb** medium-skinned person are exactly the same as the gene frequencies in the 16 children that show five different skin colors. All that *individual variation* occurs in a *group that remains constant: creation, and variation within the created kind!*

What happened as the descendants of medium-skinned parents produced a variety of descendants? Evolution? Not at all. Except for albinism (the mutational loss of skin color), the human gene pool is no bigger and no different now than the gene pool present at creation. As people multiplied, the genetic variability *built right into* the first created human beings came to visible expression. The darkest Nigerian and the lightest Norwegian, the tallest Watusi and the shortest

Pygmy, the highest soprano and the lowest bass could have been present right from the beginning in two quite average-looking people. Great variation in size, color, form, function, etc., would also be present in the two created ancestors of all the other kinds (plants and animals) as well.

Evolutionists *assume* that all life started from one or a few chemically evolved life forms with an extremely small gene pool. For evolutionists, enlargement of the gene pool by selection of random mutations is a slow, tedious process that burdens each type with a "genetic load" of harmful mutations and evolutionary leftovers. Creationists *assume* each created kind began with a large gene pool, designed to multiply and fill the earth with all its tremendous ecologic and geographic variety. (See Genesis, chapter 1.)

Neither creationist nor evolutionist was there at the beginning to see how it was done, but at least the creationist mechanism works, and it's consistent with what we observe. The evolutionist assumption *doesn't* work, and it's *not* consistent with what we presently know of genetics and reproduction. As a scientist, I prefer ideas that *do* work and *do* help to explain what we can observe, and that's creation!

According to the creation concept, each kind starts with a large gene pool present in created, probably "average-looking," parents. As descendants of these created kinds become isolated, each average-looking ("generalized") type would tend to break up into a variety of more "specialized" descendants adapted to different environments. Thus, the created ancestors of dogs, for example, have produced such varieties in nature as wolves, coyotes, and jackals. Human beings, of course, have great diversity, too. As the Bible says, God made of "one blood" (or one gene pool) all the "tribes and tongues and nations" of the earth (Fig. 21).

Varieties within a created kind have the same genes, but in different percentages. Take my ancestors, for example, the

Native Americans. Certain tribes have a high percentage of blood type **A**, but that type is quite rare among other tribes, including my branch of the Cherokee Nation. The differences represent just differences in the genes carried by the founders of each tribe as people migrated across the North American continent.

Differences from average gene percentages can come to expression quickly in small populations (a process called "genetic drift"). Take the Pennsylvania Amish, for example. Because they are descendants of only about 200 settlers who tended to marry among themselves, they have a greater percentage than their ancestors of genes for short fingers, short stature, a sixth finger, and a certain blood disease. For similar reasons, plants and animals on opposite sides of mountains, rivers, or canyons often have variations in size, color, ear-shape, or some such feature that makes them recognizable as variations of a given kind.

All the different varieties of human beings can, of course, marry one another and have children. Many varieties of plants and animals also retain the ability to reproduce and trade genes, despite differences in appearance as great as those between St. Bernards and Chihuahuas. But varieties of one kind may also lose the ability to interbreed with others of their kind. For example, fruit flies multiplying through Central and South America have split up into many subgroups (Fig. 21). And since these subgroups no longer interbreed, each can be called a separate species.

"Species" and "Kind"

Whoops! Two or more species from one kind! Isn't that evolution?

Some evolutionists certainly think so. After I participated in a creation-evolution debate at Texas A & M, a biology professor got up and told everyone about the flies on certain islands that used to interbreed but no longer do. They've

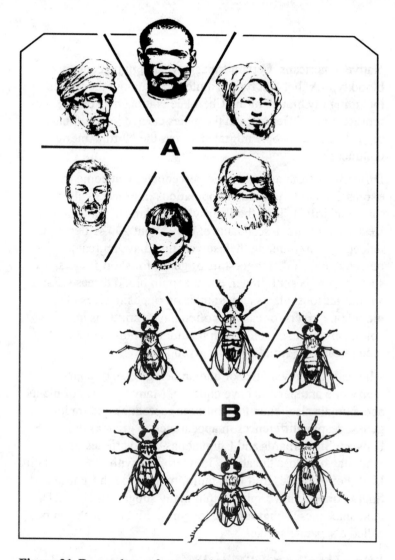

Figure 21. Descendants of created kinds tend to break up into different varieties. Even varieties that no longer interbreed (B) can be recognized as the same kind because they possess only alternate forms (alleles) of the same genes. The existence of distinct types, both living and fossil, says Harvard's Stephen Gould, "fit splendidly with creationist tenets of a pre-Darwinian era." Although Gould rejects creation, the facts seem to me to fit creation in our present "post-neo-Darwinian era" just as well.

become separate species, and that, he said, to a fair amount of applause, proves evolution is a fact—period!

Well, what about it? Barriers to reproduction do seem to arise among varieties that once interbred. Does that prove evolution? Or does that make it reasonable to extrapolate from such processes to *real* evolutionary changes from one kind to others? As I explained to the university-debate audience (also to applause), the answer is simply no, of course not. It doesn't even come close.

Any real evolution (macroevolution) requires an *expansion* of the gene pool, the *addition* of new genes and new traits as life is supposed to move from simple beginnings to ever more varied and complex forms ("molecules to man" or "fish to philosopher"). Suppose there are islands where varieties of flies that used to trade genes no longer interbreed. Is this evidence of evolution? No, exactly the opposite. Each variety resulting from reproductive isolation has a *smaller* gene pool than the original and a *restricted* ability to explore new environments with new trait combinations or to meet changes in its own environment. The long-term result? Extinction would be much more likely than evolution.

Of course, if someone insists on defining evolution as "a change in gene frequency," then the fly example "proves evolution"—but it also "proves creation," since varying the amounts of already-existing genes is what creation is all about (Fig. 22).

If evolutionists really spoke and wrote only about observable variation within kind, there would be no creation-evolution controversy. But as you know, textbooks, teachers, and television "docudramas" insist on extrapolating from simple variation within kind to the wildest sorts of evolutionary changes. And, of course, as long as they insist on such extrapolation, creationists will point out the *limits* to such change and explore creation, instead, as the more logical

117

inference from our observations. All we have ever observed is what evolutionists themselves call "subspeciation" (variation within kind), never "transspeciation" (change from one kind to others). (Fig. 22.)

Evolutionists are often asked what they mean by "species," and creationists are often asked what they mean by "kind." Creationists would like to define "kind" in terms of interbreeding, since the Bible describes different living things as "multiplying after kind," and evolutionists also use the interbreeding criterion. However, scientists recognize certain bower birds as distinct species *even though* they interbreed, and they can't use the interbreeding criterion *at all* with asexual forms. So, both creationists and evolutionists are divided into "lumpers" and "splitters." "Splitters," for example, classify cats into 28 species; "lumpers" (creationist *or* evolutionist) classify them into only one!

Perhaps each created kind is a unique combination of *non-unique* traits. Look at people, for instance. Each of us has certain traits that we may admire (or abhor): brown hair, tall stature, or even a magnificent nose like mine. Whatever the trait, someone else has exactly the same trait, but nobody has the same *combination* of traits that you do or I do. Each of us is a *unique combination* of *non-unique traits*. In a sense, that's why it's hard to classify people. If you break them up according to hair type, you'll come out with groups that won't fit with the eye type, and so on. Furthermore, we recognize *each person as distinct*.

We see a similar pattern among other living things. Each created kind is a unique combination of traits that are individually shared with members of other groups. The platypus (Fig. 9), for example, was at first considered a hoax by evolutionists, since its "weird" set of traits made it difficult even to guess what it was evolving from or into. Creationists point out that *each* of its traits (including complex ones like its electric location mechanism, leathery egg, and

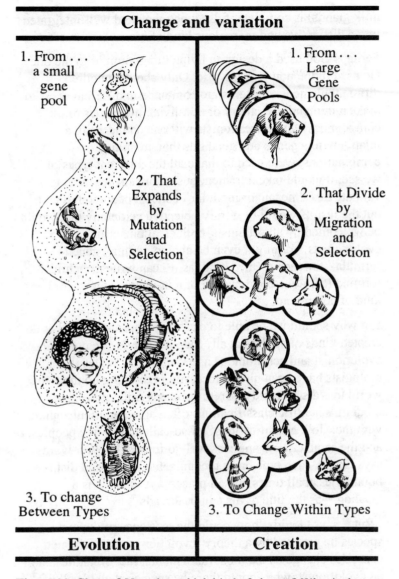

Change and variation

Evolution | **Creation**

1. From . . . a small gene pool

1. From . . . Large Gene Pools

2. That Expands by Mutation and Selection

2. That Divide by Migration and Selection

3. To change Between Types

3. To Change Within Types

Figure 22. Change? Yes—but which kind of change? What is the more logical inference, or the more reasonable extrapolation, from our observations: unlimited change from one kind to others (evolution), or limited variation within kinds (creation)? Given the new knowledge of genetics and ecology, even Darwin, I believe, would be willing to "think about it."

milk glands) is complete, fully functional, and well-integrated into a distinctive and marvelous kind of life.

Perhaps God used a design in living things similar to the one He used in the non-living world. Only about a hundred different elements or atoms are combined in different ways to make a tremendous variety of non-living molecules or compounds. Maybe creationists will one day identify a relatively few genes and gene sets that, in unique combinations, were used to make all the different types of life we see. It would take a tremendous amount of research to validate this "mosaic or modular" concept of a created unit, but the results would be a truly objective taxonomy that would be welcomed by all scientists, both creationists and evolutionists. We might even be able to write a "genetic formula" for each created kind, as we can write a chemical formula (a unique combination of non-unique atoms) for each kind of compound.

But why should we be able to classify plants and animals into created kinds or species at all? Stephen Gould,[26] eloquent evolutionist and acrimonious anti-creationist, writes that biologists have been quite successful in dividing up the living world into distinct and discrete species. Furthermore, our modern, scientific classifications often agree in minute detail with the "folk classifications" of so-called primitive peoples, and the same criteria apply as well to fossils. In other words, says Gould, each type has a recognizable reality and distinct boundaries at all times and all places: "A Quahog is a Quahog," as the title of his editorial reads.

"But," says Gould, "how could the existence of distinct species be justified by a theory [evolution] that proclaimed ceaseless change as the most fundamental fact of nature?" For an evolutionist, why should there be species at all? If all life forms have been produced by gradual expansion through selected mutations from a small beginning gene pool, organisms really should just grade into one another without distinct boundaries. Darwin also recognized the problem. He finally ended by denying the reality of species. But, as Gould points out, Darwin was quite good at *classifying* the species whose ultimate reality he denied. And, says Gould, Darwin could take no comfort in fossils, since he was also successful in classifying them into distinct species. He used the same criteria we use to classify plants and animals today.

In one of the most brilliantly and perceptively developed themes in his book *Evolution: A Theory in Crisis*, Denton[26] shows how leaders in the science of classification, after a century of trying vainly to accommodate evolution, are returning to, and fleshing out, the creationist typological concepts of the pre-Darwinian era. Indeed, the study of biological classification was founded by Karl von Linne' (Carolus Linnaeus) on the basis of his conscious and explicit Biblical belief that living things were created to multiply after kind, and that these created kinds could be rationally grouped in a hierarchical pattern reflecting themes and variations in the Creator's mind.

"Actually," concludes Gould,[28] "the existence of distinct species *was* quite consistent with *creationist* tenets of a pre-Darwinian era." (Emphasis added.) I would simply like to add that the evidence *is* also quite consistent with the creationist tenets of the present *post-neo-Darwinian* era. In Darwin's time, as well as the present, "creation" seems to be the more logical inference from our observations.

But what about Darwin? He tried to explain "design without a Designer" on the basis of selection and the inheritance of traits acquired by use and disuse (pangenes), but Pangenesis failed. The neo-Darwinists tried to explain "design without a Designer" on the basis of selection and mutation, and mutations failed. The post-neo-Darwinists are turning to "hopeful monsters," instead of simple mutations, and to "survival of the luckiest," instead of selection. These new ideas have little basis in observation or scientific principle at all, and it remains to be seen whether the evolutionist's faith in future discoveries will also fail.

One thing is for certain: If evolutionists had to prove their case in court, evolution would be thrown out for lack of evidence. That's the conclusion of two insightful lawyers, Norman MacBeth (*Darwin Retried*[29]) and Phillip Johnson (*Darwin on Trial*[30]). Neither man is arguing for the Bible; both are simply writing in their field as experts in the rules of evidence and the rules of logic. I've had the pleasure of hearing Phillip Johnson, Professor of Law at the University of California (Berkeley) challenge college students to weigh the so-called evidence for evolution and to consider alternatively the concept that life (and, hence, each of their lives) is instead the gift of Intelligent, Purposeful Design.

The evidence is forcing evolutionists to admit the severe inadequacy of mutation and selection, *but* these same processes are being picked up and used by creationists. What would Darwin say about that? Would he object to his ideas and observations being used in Biblical perspective? Darwin did muse occasionally about the role of a Creator. But, of course, we'll never know whether he would be willing to consider the Biblical framework as the more-logical inference from our present knowledge of genetics and ecology. We can be sure of this, however: A man as thoughtful and devoted to detail and observation as Darwin was, would be willing to "think about it."

Mutation-Selection in Biblical Perspective

Hold it! Mutation-selection in *Biblical* perspective? Isn't that some sort of contradiction in terms? Not at all. Like thousands of other scientists (including many evolutionists), I think the scientific evidence is quite clear: Evolution demands an increase in the quantity and quality of genetic information, and mutation-selection, *no matter how long you wait,* cannot provide it. *But, both mutation and selection are* very real, observable processes going on around us every day. *Evolution*, **no**, *but mutation-selection*, **yes**!

They don't produce evolutionary changes, but mutation and selection do indeed produce changes. Mutations are no real help in explaining the origin of *species*, but they are great for explaining the origin of disease, disease organisms, and birth defects. Natural selection is no real help in explaining the *origin* of really new species, but it's great for explaining *how* and *where* different specialized sub-types of the various created kinds "multiplied and filled the earth" after death corrupted the creation and, again, after the Flood.

I've already told you that I'm an evolutionist turned creationist, so this may surprise you: I don't believe we live in the world God created! Or, at least, we don't live in the world *as* God created it.

I've also told you I'm now the "worst kind" of creationist, a "Biblical creationist." One reason is my answer to the same problem that puzzled Darwin: how could there be so much pain, suffering, disease, death, and disaster in a world created by an all-powerful, all-loving God?

According to the Bible, God did *not* create the world full of pain and death. Instead, it was the self-centered, arrogant wickedness of human beings that ruined the world of perfect peace and harmony that God had created. In the words of Romans 8:19–21, because of man's evil, the creation was "subjected to futility. . . and a bondage to corruption." Remember, there are *four "C's" in the Biblical framework. The first, Creation, was followed by the second, Corruption.*

The Bible seems clearly to be "telling it like it is." Our world is full of far too much evidence of design, beauty, plan, and purpose to be a product of the blind processes of time, chance, and the struggle for survival. But our world is also full of too much pain, suffering, imperfection, and decay to be the work of a kindly "Mother Nature." "Nature lovers" may wish to preserve the whale and the wolf, but few are willing to push for saving the tapeworm or the AIDS virus! The rose has thorns! "Mother Nature" can be, and often is, cruel and heartless.

Our world really looks like a "corrupted creation." If you already have genes working together in coordinated sets (Creation), then random changes like mutations can produce disease, death, and other defects in design (Corruption). Like it or not, for example, our intestines are full of all kinds of bacteria. One kind makes vitamin K that assists our blood-clotting process. Many help us with digestion. In fact, if our taking antibiotics kills too many of these "good-guy" bacteria, we may suffer "intestinal distress." The cure is buttermilk or yogurt, which are nearly living things. A tablespoon of either is seething with millions of bacteria that can "re-seed" our intestines!

But what happens if radiation or a chemical accident knocks out just one of the genes in just one of these "good-guy" intestinal bacteria. That defective gene may produce a defective protein enzyme, one which is unable to complete the breakdown of some chemical. As a result of this defect, the partially broken-down chemical may be excreted by the bacterium and absorbed by the body, where it may act as a poison or toxin. You get sick, and the bacterium suffers as well (especially if you get too sick, or die and cut off its food supply!) One mutation has corrupted a created "good-guy" bacterium, turning it into a disease agent. Both host and parasite suffer, but so long as each can reproduce, life goes limping along.

"One gene-one protein" defects are also responsible for a host of hereditary diseases, some fatal and many debilitating: sickle-cell anemia, galactosemia, PKU, Tay-Sachs disease, hemophilia A, etc. And gene defects are responsible for some cancers and perhaps for some aspects of the aging process.

Time, the usual hero of the evolutionary plot, only makes matters *worse. The more time that goes by, the greater the genetic burden or genetic corruption.* Natural selection can't save us from this genetic decay, since most mutations are recessive and can sneak through a population hidden in carriers, only rarely showing up as the double recessive which can be "attacked" by natural selection. Even leading evolutionists admit that, as time goes by, accumulating genetic decay threatens the very survival of plant, animal, and human populations.

In the last chapter of their classic textbook, *Evolving: The Theory and Processes of Organic Evolution*,[30] leading evolutionists Ayala and Valentine ask the question, "What does the future hold?" When I was an evolutionist, I would have expected that chapter to be full of bright prospects: higher IQ's, greater mathematical and musical genius, faster runners and higher jumpers, nutritious and delicious foods in abundance, the conquest of disease. Instead, Ayala seems despondently concerned with basic survival: How can we save ourselves from mutations? He sees decay in genetic quality in plant, animal, and human species everywhere. He even wonders if the government might have to step in and license human reproduction, allowing couples to have children only after they pass extensive genetic tests.

What can natural selection, the evolutionist's substitute for God, do to save us from this mutational corruption? Not enough. By eliminating the worst mutations as they come to visible expression, natural selection can *slow* the process of genetic decay, but that's something like giving aspirin to a cancer patient to slow the rate of dying. Since natural selection can select only among combinations of genes that already exist or their mutational alleles, selection can no more lift us out of the quagmire of genetic decay than flapping our arms would lift us off the ground.

Darwin was certainly right about one thing: there is a struggle for survival! That comes as no surprise, of course, to a Bible student. We read about it almost right away, in the third chapter of the first book, Genesis. The first two chapters describe the perfect peace of paradise as God created it. The third chapter describes how human self-centeredness and arrogance corrupted God's creation, bringing thorns and thistles, pain, struggle, and death. But our hope is also right there in Genesis: the first promise of the salvation and restoration to new and abundant life that we have in Jesus Christ (Genesis 3:15).

Understanding the nature of mutation-selection forced me to give up the popular view called either "theistic evolution" or "progressive creation." Like most people, I grew up learning only evolution. When I became a Christian, it seemed only natural to put evolution and the Bible together. "Evolution is just God's means of creation," I told myself triumphantly. Besides that, I don't like to fight. So when I heard creationists and evolutionists arguing, I was only too happy to step in as the Great Peacemaker: "Calm down. You're both right. The Bible tells us *that* God created. Evolution tells us *how* He did it."

That's certainly an extremely popular view, and it's a temptingly easy solution. But I think many people who opt for "theistic evolution" or "progressive creation" have the same mistaken, highly romanticized concept of the evolutionary process I once had. We tend to think of evolution as just step-by-step, upward-onward progress. And that sounds like something God might do. But here's how Charles Darwin described the evolutionary process in the closing paragraphs of his *Origin of Species*:

> . . . thus, from the war of nature, famine and death, the production of higher animals directly follows.

The "*war of nature, famine, and death*." Evolution is a gruesome cycle of struggle-and-death, struggle-and-death. Unless carriers of part of a species' gene pool die, there can be no evolutionary change. Even the evolution of cooperation can proceed only over the dead bodies of all those who don't cooperate.

That's what evolutionists still believe today. Describing human origins, Carl Sagan,[31] presently the world's leading spokesman for evolution, put it this way:

> Only through an immense number of deaths of slightly maladapted organisms are you and I—brains and all—here today.

Again, death-and-accident, death-and-accident over countless generations. That's what the evolutionary process is all about. Could that be the way God created the world that He called "all very good" (Genesis 1:31)?

The more I thought about it, the more I wondered, "How could evolution be God's means of creation?" God even tells us that He was "grieved to His heart" at the "violence and corruption" that filled the earth after people turned away from Him (Genesis 6:5–6). If God was grieved by violence and corruption, how could He use it as His means of creation, or endorse it as part of a "good creation" before man ruined it? Jacques Monod, famous atheist and biochemist, once said that he was surprised that any Christian would believe that God would use such a *cruel*, *wasteful*, and *inefficient* process as evolution for His means of creation.

And why would Christ come to conquer death and to raise us to newness of life if God's plan for step-by-step improvement were based on struggle, accident, and death? Evolution is not just at odds with a verse or two in the Bible, or with someone's interpretation of the word "day." Evolution is the opposite of the whole Gospel message—the good news that death is the loser, and rich and abundant life the winner, through Jesus Christ, the Author of Life as Creator, and the Redeemer of life as our Savior!

But I haven't given up "believing in" mutation-selection! When I'm explaining how the generalized created kinds multiplied and filled the earth with variously specialized sub-types after death entered, and again after the Flood, I use natural selection (and genetic drift, gene migration, and reproductive isolation) as freely and easily as any evolutionist. And when I'm explaining the origin of disease, disease agents, and aging, I freely and easily appeal to the effects of mutations. Mutations and selection have major roles to play in the history of our planet, between its Corruption and its Restoration in Christ.

In fact, in an attempt to be as "nice" as possible, I used to say I accepted "micro-evolution," a term often given to mutation-selection working together to change the percentages of genes in a population. But then a friend cautioned me that that could be confusing. Saying I accept micro-evolution, a "little evolution," might make some think that if only I believed in enough time, a little evolution ("micro-evolution") would lead to a lot of evolution ("macro-evolution"). Nothing could be further from the truth. Even leading evolutionists now recognize that "micro" and "macro" evolution are "de-coupled," and that great variation within kind ("micro") by itself could never, even in infinite time, lead to macro-evolution.

After I explained some of these things to a hostile radio interviewer one time, he snapped, "You mean evolution explains the bad changes and creation explains the good changes." With a smile he did not find appealing, I replied: "Yes! You've got it!"

But let me add one more thing. After a lecture in which I was describing the depressing decline in genetic quality resulting from the continuous build-up of harmful mutations, someone asked plaintively, "Isn't there some good news in all these gene combinations?" And there is. With God, as with us created in His image, "variety is the spice of life." God seems to have endowed the first of each created kind with dazzling genetic variability and the Hardy-Weinberg Law, the fundamental law of population genetics, acts to conserve that created variability. God created just two people, for example, with all the genes needed to produce children dark and light, tall and short, bass and soprano, etc.!

That means each child is an absolutely unique, never-to-be-repeated combination of traits. There's a children's song, "God made me special; I'm the only one of my kind." And that is true!! *Each person is a treasure, with a place in God's plan that no one else can take.*

And that's not all. To the extent that these things depend on gene combinations, we may not yet have seen the greatest mathematical or musical genius, the fastest runner or highest jumper, the most skilled artist or craftsman. God's plan at creation is still unfolding before our very eyes. That's not evolution (adding something not there before); that's "entelechy"— creativity written ahead of time in the fabulous genetic code of DNA! Maybe it's time we treated each other as the miraculous marvels we are! THINK ABOUT IT!

End Notes

1 Kelly, Thomas (producer). *Puzzle of the Ancient Wing*. Canadian Broadcasting Corporation., "Man Alive" television series. 1981.

2 Durant, Will. "Historian Will Durant: We Are in the Last Stage of Pagan Period." *El Cajon (CA) Daily Californian*, 8, April, 1980 (by Rogers Worthington of *The Chicago Tribune*).

3 Osborne, Chris D. *A Reevaluation of the Engilish Peppered Moth's Use as an Example of Evolution in Progress*. "Master's Thesis, Institute for Creation Research, Santee, CA. 1985.

4 Dobzhansky, Theodosius, F. Ayala, L. Stebbins, and J. Valentine. *Evolution*. San Francisco: W. H. Freeman and Co. 1977.

5 Lester, Lane, and Ray Bohlin. *The Natural Limits to Biological Change*. Grand Rapids: Zondervan. 1984.

6 Gould, Stephen Jay. "The Return of Hopeful Monsters." *Natural History*, June/July 1977.

7 Gould, Stephen Jay. "Of Turtles, Vets, Elephants, and Castles." *New Scientist*, January 11, 1979.

8 Lewontin, Richard C. "Adaptation." *Scientific American* (and *Scientific American*. book *Evolution*). September. 1978.

9 Novick, Richard. "Plasmids." *Scientific American*, December 1980.

10 Moorehead, Paul S., and Martin M. Kaplan. *Mathematical Challenges to the Neo-Darwinian Interpretation of Evolution*. Wistar Symposium No. 5. Philadelphia: Wistar Institute Press. 1967.

11 Denton, Michael. *Evolution: A Theory in Crisis*. London: Burnett Books. 1985.

12 Dobzhansky, Theodosius, F. Ayala, L. Stebbins, and J. Valentine. *Evolution*. San Francisco: W. H. Freeman and Co. 1977.

13 Ayala, Francisco. "The Mechanisms of Evolution." *Scientific American* (and *Scientific American* book *Evolution*). September 1978.

14 Beadle, George W. "The Ancestry of Corn." *Scientific American*, January 1980.

15 Ayala, Francisco. "The Mechanisms of Evolution." *Scientific American* (and *Scientific American* book, *Evolution*) September 1978.

16 Gould, Stephen Jay. "The Return of Hopeful Monsters." *Natural History*, June/July 1977.

17 Gould, Stephen Jay. "Is a New General Theory of Evolution Emerging?" *Paleobiology*, Winter 1980.

18 Adler, Jerry and John Carey. "Is Man a Subtle Accident?" *Newsweek*, November 3, 1980.

19 Lewin, Roger. "Evolutionary Theory Under Fire." *Science*, November 21, 1980.

20 Patterson, Colin. Address at American Museum of Natural History. New York. November 5, 1981.

21 Kelly, Thomas (producer). *Puzzle of the Ancient Wing*. Canadian Broadcasting Corporation, "Man Alive" television series, 1981.

22 Grasse', Pierre Paul. *Evolution of Living Organisms*. New York: Academic Press, 1977.

23 Ayala, Francisco. "The Mechanisms of Evolution." *Scientific American* (and *Scientific American* book *Evolution*). September 1978.

24 Parker, Gary, E. Reynolds, W. Ann Reynolds, and Rex Reynolds. *Heredity*. Rev. ed. Programmed Biology Series. Chicago: Educational Methods, Inc. 1977.

25 Gould, Stephen Jay. "A Quahog is a Quahog." *Natural History*, August/September 1979. Also published August 2, 1979 in *New Scientist* as "Species Are Not Specious."

26 Denton, Michael. *Evolution: A Theory in Crisis*. London: Burnett Books. 1985. Chapters 5-9.

27 Gould, Stephen Jay. "A Quahog is a Quahog." *Natural History*, August/September 1979. Also published August 2, 1979 in *New Scientist* as "Species Are Not Specious."

28 MacBeth, Norman. *Darwin Retried*. Boston: Gambit. 1971.

29 Johnson, Phillip. *Darwin on Trial*, Washington D. C.: Regnery Gateway. 1991.

30 Ayala, Francisco, and James W. Valentine. *Evolving: The Theory and Processes of Organic Evolution*. Menlo Park: Benjamin-Cummins Publishing Company. 1979.

31 Sagan, Carl. "A Gift for Vividness." As quoted in *Time*, October 20, 1980. page 68.

32 Ham, Ken. *The Lie: Evolution*. Master Books, Colorado Springs, Colorado. 1987.

Chapter 3

The Fossil Evidence

Introduction

The Canadian Broadcasting Corporation (CBC) produced a program involving the creation-evolution question. Tom Kelly, its producer, invited me along with other scientists to be filmed as part of the program. The result was one of the fairest, most enlightening, and well-produced programs ever done by the public media on the subject of origins.[1]

Most encouraging was the letter I received from Tom, especially this section:

> For the record, I went into the program as an evolutionist, without knowing why or quite what that meant. By the time I had done the research, of one thing I was sure, that if evolution is true, the chance-and-time process just does not *work*!"

Time, chance, and struggle are supposed to be the force behind evolution, but a large and increasing number of scientists, scholars, and ordinary thoughtful people are coming to Tom Kelly's conclusion: ". . . the chance-and-time process just does not *work*!" The "evolutionary engine" has no power.

But many who agree that science has not shown *how* evolution could occur still believe that evolution is a fact! How can that be? The answer in a word: *fossils*.

Now I've ruined everything! If only I hadn't mentioned fossils, maybe I could have convinced you that the evidence we've looked at (biochemistry, embryology, homology, ecology, genetics, adaptation, classification, variation) really supports plan, purpose, and special acts of creation, not time, chance, and evolutionary struggle. But if we're going to honestly "think about it," we've got to include fossils.

Fossils used to scare me. After my heart and mind were opened to consider the Biblical framework for origins in contrast to evolution, I gradually convinced myself (over a three-year period!) that the evidence in *biology* overwhelmingly favored the Biblical view. But friends knew how to stop me cold: "Look, Parker, if you only knew anything about fossils (paleontology), then you'd give up this creationist nonsense and come on back into the 20th century with the rest of us!" I even began to wonder whether some parts of the Bible and evolution could *still* be made to fit together—"progressive creation" maybe?

About that time, God did something wonderful for me. I got a grant from the National Science Foundation for 15 months of full-time work on my doctoral degree. To my major in biology, I added a cognate in geology, emphasizing the study of fossils and origins. I had done my master's degree work as a practicing atheist and evolutionist. Now, I was sure I was a Christian, and I leaned toward creation, but if the fossils didn't work out, I just wouldn't talk about creation any more.

Well, I fell in love with fossils. My family and I (that's two rock hounds and four pebble pups!) have collected oodles of fossils from numerous sites in America, Canada, and Australia, and a few spots in Europe and Asia, and I regularly lead university students in field-study courses to Grand Canyon and to well-known fossil sites.

Fossils are the remains or traces of once-living things preserved largely in sedimentary deposits. They represent the closest we can come to *historical* evidence in this matter of origins, so they are of prime importance in comparing Biblical and evolutionary pictures of history (perhaps even forcing some sort of blending of the two?)

Actually, fossils can help us with two types of questions: First, *what kinds* of plants and animals once populated the earth? Second, *how fast* were fossils, and the rock layers that contain them, formed?

I. WHAT KINDS?

When the modern version of the creation-evolution dialogue got started in the middle of the last century, creationists and evolutionists had radically different ideas of the kinds of life they expected to find as fossils.

The evolutionist, of course, expected to find fossils that showed stages through which one kind of animal or plant changed into a different kind. According to evolution, the boundaries between kinds should blur as we look further and further back into their fossil history. It should get more and more difficult, for example, to tell cats from dogs and then mammals from reptiles, land animals from water animals, and finally life from non-life. They expected also that the criteria we use to classify plants and animals today would be less and less useful as older and older fossils showed the in-between characteristics of presumed common ancestors for different groups.

But if the different kinds of life we see today are the descendants of created kinds, as the creationist says, then all we ought to find as fossils are just *variations of these kinds*, with decline and even extinction evident as a result of corruption and the catastrophe of Noah's Flood. The same kind of criteria we use to classify plants and animals today ought to work just as well with fossils, and each kind should represent a mosaic of complete traits.

Certainly, the evolutionist and the creationist had radically different concepts of what would be found, as the systematic study of fossils began in earnest in the middle of the last century. Let's take a look now at the evidence. Which concept does it support—evolution, or the Biblical framework of Creation-Corruption-Catastrophe-Christ?

Invertebrates: Animals Without Backbones

Take a look at Fig. 23. If you live near the seashore or like to visit marine aquaria, I'm sure most of the animals there are quite familiar to you. There are some jellyfish floating in the background. On the bottom, you can find sea urchins and sea lilies, members of the starfish group; a couple of snails; sponges; lampshells; and members of the earthworm group. That large fellow stretched out along the right side is a nautiloid, a squid-like animal that is a member of the most complex group of invertebrate animals we know anything about (the cephalopod mollusks). The nautiloid belongs to the group of animals that has an eye somewhat like ours, as I mentioned in the first chapter.

What does this illustration show? A picture of present-day sea life off the Florida coast or around some tropical island? No, not at all. It pictures *not* sea life today, but the "first" or simplest community of plants and animals to leave abundant fossil remains. This illustration shows life in the so-called "Age of Trilobites" (what I'll later call the "Zone of Trilobites").

Trilobites, by the way, are fascinating creatures. Many trilobites, such as the one pictured in the inset in Fig. 23, had extremely complex eyes. When I take students snorkeling and scuba diving, I have to warn them that organisms and objects underwater appear closer and larger than they really are (so that big, nearby shark is really smaller and farther away!) Some trilobites didn't have that problem. They had double-lens systems that made the corrections for underwater vision, sort of "hand-crafted prescription face masks," masterpieces of design.

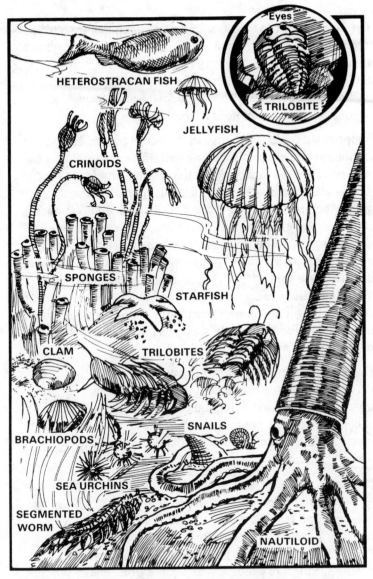

Figure 23. The "first" or simplest community to leave abundant fossils, the lower "Trilobite Seas" (Cambrian System), contains almost all the major groups of sea life, including the most complex invertebrates, the nautiloids, and the highly complex trilobites (inset above). Darwin called the fossil evidence "perhaps the most obvious and serious objection to the theory" of evolution.

Trilobites belong to the same complex group that insects do (the arthropods). Unfortunately, no trilobites are known to be alive today. Trilobites are very famous as fossils, however, and may have a lot to tell us about how life began. As my paleontology professor, an evolutionist, said: "Never let anyone tell you a trilobite is a simple animal."

Suppose we could scuba dive in the ocean back when the trilobites were alive. If we compared life in the trilobite seas with what we see in the oceans today, what would we say? "Look at all the new forms of life, the increased variety and greater complexity!" No, that's not what we would say at all. Rather, we might say, "What happened? Where did everything go? What happened to all the trilobites? Where are all the lampshells? There used to be several thousand species of lampshells (brachiopods); now only a handful are left!" We might also wonder what happened to the great nautiloids, so much bigger and more varied in the Cambrian seas than those today. Today, the only shelled squid we have is the modest pearly nautilus.

Decline and even extinction, *not* evolution, is the rule when we compare fossil sea life with the sort of marine invertebrates we find living today. In fact, all major groups, except perhaps the groups including clams and snails, are represented by *greater variety* and *more complex* forms as *fossils* than today.

It's hard to imagine how absolutely crushing this evidence is to evolution. Suppose, for example, that you had a burning desire to find out where snails came from. You search the fossil evidence all over the world, all the way back to the "beginning," the "first" abundant fossils in Cambrian deposits, and, sure enough, snails come from snails. Where did the most complex of all the invertebrates, members of the squid and octopus group, the cephalopods, come from? Again, you search through all the fossil evidence, all the way back to the very "beginning," and, sure enough, "squids" come from

138

"squids." In fact, the first "squids" (cephalopods), the nautiloids, are more impressive than most modern forms. And, of course, trilobites seem only to come from trilobites. There's no evidence they evolved from, or into, anything else.

In other words, you find snails and squids and trilobites as fossils; you don't find "snids" and "squails" and "squailobites," or some other in-between form or common ancestor. The "missing links" between these groups are *still* missing.

In fact, few scientists, if any, are still looking for fossil links between the major invertebrate groups. The reason is simple. All the groups appear as separate, distinct, diversified lines in the deepest fossil-rich deposits. Evolutionists are well aware of these facts, of course, and several have admitted that this "explosion" of life in Cambrian ("lower trilobite") rock seems to favor the concept of creation.

The sudden appearance of a multitude of complex and varied life forms at the very bottom of the fossil-rich portion of the geologic column is now routinely called the "Cambrian explosion." A far greater variety of basic body plans is present among Cambrian fossils than among life forms along Australia's Great Barrier Reef, perhaps the richest life zone today! Evolutionists had expected life to begin with a few simple life forms thrown together by time, chance, and chemistry, and they had expected the variety and complexity of life to build gradually as natural selection culled the best from random mutational changes. Although it's still taught, the Cambrian evidence renders this classic view flatly false!

To a creationist, Cambrian fossils are simply the descendants of the created (and corrupted) kinds first buried in the catastrophe of Noah's Flood. When I was a graduate student trying to decide between creation and evolution, the Cambrian fossil evidence made it very hard to believe in evolution, very easy to accept what the Bible says about Creation, Corruption, Catastrophe, and Christ.

Evolutionists have come up with just about every explanation for the Cambrian explosion *except* the Biblical model. Francis Crick, the Nobel laureate who argued chemical evolution was impossible on earth and must have occurred on another planet, followed up by suggesting that the "seeds of life" arrived on earth in some sort of rocket ship that accidentally or deliberately hit the earth, giving life an explosive extra-terrestrial "jump start."

Many evolutionists still cling to their traditional belief that life did start slowly and gradually on earth, but that the *evidence rotted away* since the early forms lacked the hard parts that make the best fossils. The Cambrian explosion, then, is simply an explosion of hard parts occurring simultaneously in many different animal groups. Besides being *an appeal to faith* rather than *an inference from science*, the "hard part hypothesis" requires multiple mathematical miracles for the repeated origin of gene sets for hard parts by time-and-chance in different lines. The view also contradicts the most reasonable of all evolutionary assumptions, that complex features, like hard parts, have descended by variation from a common ancestor in which the feature originated by just one "miracle," not many miracles after the lines diverged.

The hard-part hypothesis also contradicts the fossil evidence. Although rare, soft parts *do preserve*, and, although rare, Precambrian fossils *are found*. What does the Precambrian soft-part evidence tell us about life before the Cambrian deposits were laid down?

Evolutionists used to say that they would have found the ancestors of Cambrian life there if only the evidence hadn't rotted or been destroyed by heat in the rocks. That "excuse" no longer works. Although most Precambrian rock is the igneous and metamorphic type unsuitable for fossil preservation, we have now discovered great stretches of Precambrian sedimentary rocks that could and should have preserved soft parts and the common ancestors of the diverse and complex Cambrian life— *if* any such evolutionary ancestors existed.

Actually, Precambrian fossils strongly support the creation concept. My wife, Mary, and I have found soft-bodied jellyfish and members of the earthworm group (annelids) in the famous Ediacara beds of South Australia. What lessons do we learn from the "oldest" animal fossils? Once a jellyfish, always a jellyfish; once an "earthworm" (annelid), always an "earthworm." Most people think of segmented worms as fish bait, but to a biologist, they are marvelously complex. The "lowly" earthworm, for example, has five "hearts," a two-hemisphere brain, and a multi-organed digestive system. It looks like Precambrian animal fossils are telling us the same thing about the origin of life that Cambrian fossils are: Living things look as if they were created well designed to multiply after their kinds and to fill the earth with stupendous and soul-satisfying variety!

Creation is also supported by our ability to use the same criteria to classify both living plants and animals and those found as fossils. Even among extinct types, we don't find "in-between forms," or forms that are any harder to classify (when the fossil evidence is complete enough) than plants and animals living today.

Most people just assume that fossils and evolution go hand in hand. Some people even seem to think that "believing in" fossils is almost the same as "believing in" evolution. We've been so thoroughly indoctrinated with "educational" materials and entertainment touting evolution, that it's hard even to think that fossils argue so strongly *against* evolution and *for* the Biblical outline of history.

Could I be right about that? Is there anyone else who thinks that the fossils argue *against* evolution? Yes, indeed . . . Charles Darwin, for one. That's right, Charles Darwin, the father of the modern concept of evolution. Darwin thought that the fossil evidence was "perhaps the most obvious and serious objection which could be urged against the theory [of evolution]." Why? Because he knew some of the same things that we know about fossils.

Darwin's chapter on the fossil evidence was titled "On the Imperfection of the Geologic Record." In that chapter he dealt with "the sudden appearance" of groups of fossils in the lowest known fossil-bearing strata (the Cambrian). When it came to intermediate links (those types of fossils supposed to show how one kind of life evolved into others), Darwin wrote the following:

> . . . intermediate links? Geology assuredly does *not* reveal any such finely graduated organic change, and this is perhaps the *most obvious and serious objection* which can be urged against the theory [of evolution]. [Emphasis added.]

So Darwin was faced with a conflict. Theory (evolution) and facts (fossils) didn't agree. Which was he going to throw out, the facts or the theory? Darwin chose to throw out the facts. *Normally*, of course, a scientist doesn't do that. But Darwin had reason, or at least hope, for doing so. He blamed the conflict between fact and theory on "the imperfection of the geologic record." In his time, the science of paleontology (fossil study) was just getting under way. He hoped that as new fossil evidence was unearthed around the world, the "missing links" would be found to support his theory.

But, it's now well over a century since Darwin made that statement, and we've unearthed thousands of tons of fossils from all over the world. What does all this massive amount of evidence show? Have we found the "missing links" required to support the theory of evolution, or have we merely unearthed further evidence of variation within the created kinds?

David Raup reviews the evidence for us. He has been the curator of the famous Field Museum of Natural History in Chicago. That museum houses 20% of all fossil species known, so Raup is in a position to speak with considerable knowledge about the fossil evidence. The title of his article in the *Field Museum Bulletin* is "Conflicts Between Darwin and Paleontology," and the thrust is repeated and expanded in a second article.[2,3]

Raup starts by saying that "most people assume that fossils provide a very important part of the general argument made in favor of Darwinian interpretations of the history of life. Unfortunately, this is not strictly true." He then quotes the same passage from Darwin that I did, and points out that Darwin was "embarrassed" by the fossil evidence. He goes on to say that we now have a rich body of fossil knowledge, so that we can no longer blame the conflict between evolutionary theory and the fossil facts on the "imperfection of the geologic record." He mentions also, as I did, that Darwin expected those gaps in his theory, those missing links, to be unearthed by future discoveries. Then Raup summarizes those discoveries:

> Well, we are now about 120 years after Darwin, and knowledge of the fossil record has been greatly expanded . . . Ironically, we have *even fewer examples* of evolutionary transition than we had in Darwin's time. By this I mean that some of the classic cases of Darwinian change in the fossil record, such as the evolution of the horse in North America, have had to be *discarded* or *modified* as a result of more detailed information. [Emphasis added.]

What a statement! Darwin said that the fossil evidence was perhaps the most obvious and serious objection against his theory. Raup is saying that 120 years of research have made the case for Darwinian evolution *even worse*. Raup says we have "even fewer examples" now, since new evidence has forced evolutinists to change their minds about examples, like the horse, that were once used. (For details, see the masters thesis by Walter Barnhart,[4] a student of mine, and the book by Gish.[5])

Raup goes on to say that "we still have a record which *does* show change, but one that can hardly be looked upon as the most reasonable consequence of natural selection." In comparing fossil forms with modern forms, we do see change all right, but it's *not* the kind of change associated with natural selection. It's simply *variation within the created kinds*, plus decline and even extinction, reflecting corruption and catastrophe.

Raup is still an evolutionist, but he's beginning to argue for "survival of the luckiest," instead of "survival of the fittest." Condemning with faint praise, he says, "natural selection as a process is okay. We are also pretty sure that it goes on in nature, although good examples are surprisingly rare." Genetic studies suggest that mutation-selection *could not* lead to evolutionary change; the fossil evidence seems to confirm that it *did not*.

Raup then tries to argue that "optimal engineering design" is the best evidence of evolution—exactly the same kind of evidence that Harvard geneticist Lewontin concedes as the best evidence of *creation*! One of the reasons evolution continues to survive is that paleontologists believe geneticists have the real evidence, and geneticists believe that paleontologists have the evidence, and so on around the various specialties within biology, each man passing the buck for evidence to the next man. Since professionals in different disciplines rarely talk with one another about such matters, the *myth* of overwhelming support for evolution continues.

After he bemoaned the repeated failures of evolution to come to grips with the fossil evidence, paleontologist Niles Eldredge[6] laments that the only alternative is "Special Creation." As we have seen, the fossils of invertebrates, the most abundant by far of all fossils, *do* offer strong support for the concept of creation, specifically the Biblical concepts of Creation-Corruption-Catastrophe-Christ. But let's look now at fossil evidence from other groups.

Fossil Plants

Did you even wonder what kind of plants the dinosaurs tromped around on? The answer may surprise you. Some of these unfamiliar animals wandered around among some very familiar plants: oak, willow, magnolia, sassafras, palms, and other such common flowering plants.

In the geologic sequence, the flowering plants first appear suddenly and in great diversity in Cretaceous ("upper dinosaur") rock. Darwin was aware of the situation and called the origin of these plants "an abominable mystery." As my professor of paleobotany summarized it, nothing has happened in the last century or so to solve that mystery. As far as the fossil evidence is concerned, we simply find different varieties of the same types of plants we have today, plus decline and/or extinction in many cases.

There is a tendency to give every different fossil fragment a different scientific genus-species name. Five different genus names were given to fossil specimens that later turned out to be parts of just *one* type of tree, the *Lepidodendron*. But many of the flowering plants are so easily recognizable that they are classified using the same scientific names we use today.

Other fossil plants are as easily classified as the flowering plants. The ferns and fern allies appear suddenly and simultaneously in Silurian/Devonian rock in far greater diversity than we have today (Fig. 24). Yet none of these fossil plants has any features of anatomy, morphology, or reproduction that are hard to understand in terms of what we observe among living plants. The difference is this: There used to be many more kinds of ferns and fern allies on the earth than there are today. And some of these that are small and inconspicuous today, like the "ground pine" (*Lycopodium*) and "horsetail" (*Equisetum*), had fossils with similar parts that grew to be huge trees (e.g., *Lepidodendron* and *Calamites*, respectively). The structural design and classification of plants seem to point to Creation; the decline in size and variety to the Corruption and Catastrophe that followed.

Even the algae are recognizable from their first appearance in the fossil sequence as greens, blue-greens, reds, browns, and yellow-browns, the same groups we have today. The "oldest" fossils found so far are some Precambrian blue-green algae that form rocky structures called stromatolites. (I've had the privilege of examining and photographing these on both the west and south coasts of Australia.) Are these algae "simple" forms of life like evolutionists had hoped to find? Exactly the opposite! When it comes to energy biochemistry, those "simple" algae are more complex than we are. They can take sea water and turn it into living cells, using just sunlight for energy—a *fantastically* intricate feat of biochemical engineering called photosynthesis. (Don't you wish we could run on just water, air, and sunlight!)

Blue-green algal stomatolites are also found living the same way just offshore from their "old" Precambrian fossils. What's the lesson from these "oldest" plant fossils? Evolution—change from simple beginnings to more complex and varied kinds? Not at all. The lesson from the "oldest" plant fossils seems to be the same as that from the "oldest"

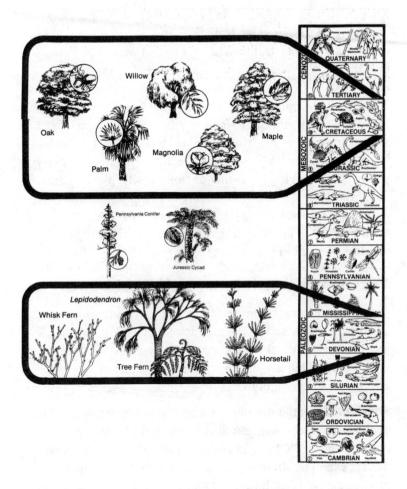

Figure 24. Fossil plants are easily classified using the same criteria we use today and, perhaps because of extinction following the Flood, we find even greater variation among fossil plants than we find now. As Professor Corner of Cambridge put it, " . . . to the unprejudiced, the fossil record of plants is in favor of special creation."

animal fossils: Living things were created complex and well designed to multiply after kind.

My paleobotany professor (an evolutionist) started his class by saying he supposed we were there to learn about the evolution of plants. But then he told us that we weren't going to learn much. What we *would* learn, he said, is that our modern plant groups go way back in their fossil history. Sure enough, all we studied was "petrified plant anatomy," features already familiar to me from the study of living plants. We encountered some difficulties in classification, of course, but only the same kinds which we encounter among the *living* plants. Summarizing the evidence from fossils' plant studies, E. J. H. Corner, Professor of Botany at Cambridge University, once put it this way (even though *he* believed in their evolution): ". . . to the unprejudiced, the fossil record of plants is in favor of special creation."

Vertebrates: Animals with Backbones

But when we come to the vertebrates, the animals with backbones, the situation changes dramatically. We run smack into the most powerful evidence of *evolution*. At least that's what I used to tell my students when I taught university biology as an evolutionist.

Sometimes I would run into a student who would ask me, "If evolution is true, where are the missing links?" "Missing links?" I'd say. "Glad you asked. It just so happens we have a perfect example: *Archaeopteryx*, the link that shows how reptiles evolved into birds!"

Archaeopteryx is *the* showcase for evolution. There is only one really photogenic specimen, the Berlin specimen, which is pictured in essentially all biology textbooks. That specimen, along with a reconstruction in the same position, is shown in Fig. 25.

Reconstruction

Fossil Specimen

Figure 25. At last—evidence of evolution! . . . *or is it*? The famous *Archaeopteryx* combines features most often found in reptiles (teeth, claws, unfused vertebrae, and a long bony tail) with features distinctive of birds (wings, feathers, and a furcula or wishbone). Does *Archaeopteryx* provide clues as to how scales evolved into feathers, or legs into wings? Is *Archaeopteryx* more likely an evolutionary link, *or* a mosaic of complete traits (a distinctive created kind)? Read both sides and think about it.

At first, you may wonder what the fuss is all about. It has feathers, wings, and a beak, so it's a bird. But look closer. It has teeth in the bill, claws on the wings, no keel on the breast bone, an unfused backbone, and a long, bony tail. These are all characteristics we normally associate with reptiles. What's more, the existence of a creature like *Archaeopteryx* was predicted by evolutionists before any such specimen was found! What's a creationist going to say to a "perfect example of evolution" like *Archaeopteryx*? There's no way I can get you to consider creation without facing up to *Archaeopteryx*.

Well, first of all, the reptile-like features are not really as reptile-like as you might suppose. The familiar ostrich, for example, has claws on its wings that are even *more* "reptile-like" than those of *Archaeopteryx*. Several birds, such as the hoatzin, don't have much of a keel. The penguin has unfused backbones and a bony tail. No living birds have socketed teeth, but some fossil birds do. Besides, some reptiles have teeth and some don't, so presence or absence of teeth is not particularly important in distinguishing the two groups.

More importantly, take a look at the individual features of *Archaeopteryx*. Is there any clue as to how legs evolved into wings? No, none at all. When we find wings as fossils, we find *completely developed, fully functional wings*. That's true of *Archaeopteryx*, and it's also true of the flying insects, flying reptiles (pterodactyls), and the flying mammals (bats).

Is there any clue in *Archaeopteryx* as to *how* reptilian scales evolved into feathers? No, none at all. When we find feathers as fossils, we find *fully developed and functional feathers*. Feathers are quite complex structures, with little hooks and eyelets for zippering and unzippering them. *Archaeopteryx* not only had complete and complex feathers, but feathers of several different types! As a matter of fact, it had the asymmetric feather characteristic of strong fliers. An evolutionist once claimed that penguin wings showed the transition from scale to feather. Their small feathers do overlap like scales (or roofing shingles!), but their microstructure and development are 100% feather. He might as well have claimed the feathers evolved from shingles!

What about lack of a keel? Actually, muscles for the power stroke in flight attach to the wishbone or furcula, and *Archaeopteryx* had "an extremely robust furcula." As a matter of fact, a growing number of evolutionists, perhaps a consensus, now believe that *Archaeopteryx* was a strong flier. Many now consider *Archaeopteryx* the first bird, and not a missing link between reptiles and birds (See Denton,[8] and Wiford[9]). (A few scientists, including Sir Fred Hoyle, think *Archaeopteryx* is a hoax. See Ian Taylor,[10] for discussion.)

Actually the final piece in the *Archaeopteryx* puzzle (for the time being, anyway) has been put into place with the discovery in Texas of a quarry full of bird bones ("proto-avis"), entombed in rock layers much "deeper" than those which contain *Archaeopteryx* remains. What does that mean? It simply means that the *Archaeopteryx* specimens *we have* cannot have been the ancestors of birds, because birds *already existed*.

Evolutionists who accept *Archaeopteryx* as a bird must, of course, look elsewhere for the ancestors of birds. The new candidate is called "pro-avis" (which is *not* the same as the Texas birds loosely called "proto-avis"). John Ostrom[11] of Yale University discusses two possible pictures of this pro-avis, as re-drawn in Fig. 26. One hypothesis has birds starting as partially feathered reptiles gliding down from trees. Ostrom points out a number of anatomical inconsistencies in that view. He then suggests that birds began as two-legged reptiles, with feathery baskets on their forearms, that jumped higher and higher to catch flying insects.

Take a look at the idea of pro-avis in Fig. 26-B. Can you see any problems in getting it off the ground? Perhaps you've

Figure 26. Two concepts of the evolutionary ancestor of birds, called "pro-avis," are redrawn here from an article by Yale's John Ostrom. As Ostrom says, "No fossil evidence of any pro-avis exists. It is a purely hypothetical pre-bird, but one which must have existed." But this case for evolution is based on *faith,* not *facts.* The fossils found so far simply show that birds have always been birds, of many distinctive kinds.

seen children tie towels onto their arms and try to fly. If you ever tried it yourself (as I once did), you found that all that flapping created more drag than lift! Even though it's his idea, Ostrom acknowledges that the muscle action for catching insects is all wrong for flying. And eating insects out of the feathers would tear up the feathers anyway.

Besides these difficulties, Ostrom also points out that "No fossil evidence exists of any pro-avis. It is a purely hypothetical pre-bird, but one that must have existed." Apparently, where facts fail, faith avails! Ostrom and other evolutionists can be commended for their imagination. But their ideas cannot be presented in science classrooms as logical inferences from observed data, since they admit themselves *the data simply do not exist.*

As far as the fossil evidence is concerned, different kinds of invertebrates and plants have always been different kinds of invertebrates and plants. . . and birds have always been birds. The fossil evidence of creation is just as clear in the other vertebrate groups as well (See Gish[12] and see Bliss, Parker, and Gish[13]). It seems to me that "creation" is clearly the logical inference from our scientific knowledge of fossils.

During the late '70's and early '80's, a group of evolutionists led by Harvard's Stephen Gould tried to resurrect the idea that evolution happened in big jumps, "The Return of Hopeful Monsters" Gould called it.[14] The hopeful-monster idea (variously expressed as punctuated equilibrium, saltatory evolution, or quantum speciation) was proposed to explain why the links required by gradual evolution have never been found. But the "big jumpers" were never able to explain how these big jumps could occur genetically, nor could they answer this crucial question about the first appearance of any hopeful-monster: *with what would it mate?*

At least the creationist and the post-neo-Darwinian punctuationalist *agree that the missing links are missing.* But

Figure 27 Harvard's Stephen Gould says that, "The fossil record with its abrupt transitions offers no support for gradual change . . . ." He proposes instead that evolution occurs in jumps by the "rare success of those hopeful monsters." Could a bird, for example, hatch from a *reptile's egg*? Gould assumes a materialistic philosophy for himself and all other scientists, however, and that does not permit him to consider creation as a more-logical inference from the fossil evidence.

what is the scientific difference between saying that the missing links can never be found (the "new" evolution) and saying that they never existed at all (creation)?

Sometimes it's kind of fun to be a creationist. The "rear-guard" neo-Darwinian evolutionists like to point out the apparent absurdity of hopeful-monster evolution and claim that *evolution could not happen fast*. The punctuational evolutionists point to genetic limits and the fossil evidence to show that *evolution did not happen slowly*. The creationist simply agrees with both sides: Evolution couldn't happen fast, and it didn't happen slowly—because evolution can't and didn't happen at all! In terms of the kind of variation that *can* and *did* occur, the creation concept seems to be the far more logical inference from our observations.

At least the hopeful monster concept avoids the problem of missing links. But notice: this alternate concept of *evolution* is based on the fossils we *don't find* and on genetic mechanisms that have *never been observed*. The case for *creation* is based on thousands of tons of fossils that we *have found* and on genetic mechanisms (variation within kind) that we *do observe* and see occuring every day. As a scientist, I prefer a model that's based on what we *do* see and *can* explain (creation), rather than one that's based on what we *don't* see and *cannot* explain (evolution).

Human Beings

What about ourselves? What can we infer from the evidence regarding the origin of human beings? Evolutionists now give us two choices.[15] Either human beings are the result of time, chance, and a ceaseless struggle for survival, or else we began as "a hopeful monster whose star was a bit more benevolent than most." According to creationists, the evidence suggests, instead, that we are here by the plan, purpose, and special creative acts of God.

I've mentioned being part of a television program on creation-evolution produced by the secular Canadian Broadcasting Corporation (CBC).[16] The program opened with a medieval princess wandering in a castle garden, apparently looking for something. Then the camera panned over to a rock ledge around a pond. There it was, big bulging eyes and all: a frog. Right before our incredulous eyes, the princess leaned over and kissed the frog. Stars sparkled across the TV screen, then a handsome prince appeared. As the prince and princess embraced, the narrator stepped into the scene with this introduction: If you believe a frog turns into a prince instantly, that's a fairy tale; if you believe a frog turns into a prince in 300 million years, that's evolution.

When I believed and taught evolution, I would not have put it that way, or course. But as I look back, I realize *that* story reflects what I really was teaching. According to evolution, if you simply wait long enough, time, chance, and struggle (mutation and selection) will gradually turn some amphibians, like that frog, into reptiles, mammals, apes, and finally man, like that prince.

Scientists can understand how a "machine" with as many complex and interdependent parts as a human being could be put together by intelligent creative design. Could chance and struggle over vast amounts of time do the same thing without any outside help and no planning ahead? Nothing in our scientific experience suggests time and chance have that kind of creative ability, although much of our common experience demonstrates that time and chance can *destroy* design! To convince scientists and skeptics, then, clearly the *burden of proof lies with the evolutionist* to find a series of fossils suggesting the change from frog to prince, or at least ape to man.

The first fossils proposed as links between apes and mankind were the "cave men" called Neanderthals. Neanderthal was originally portrayed as a "beetle-browed, barrel-chested, bow-legged brute" (a suitable ancestor for a mugger, if nothing else!) The creationists in those days responded, "Hey, wait a minute. Neanderthals are just plain people, some of whom suffered bone diseases." The first Neanderthals discovered, came from harsh inland environments in Europe, where they could easily have (like many of our own American-plains Indians) suffered skeletal abnormalities, especially from lack of iodine in the diet and shortage of sun-induced vitamin D necessary for calcium absorption during the long winters.

Neanderthals from the Palestine area do not show the more stooped and massive features. The brain volume of Neanderthals is slightly *larger* than the average brain volume of people today, and Neanderthal peoples had a well-developed culture, art, and religion. Nowadays, evolutionists agree completely with creationists: Neanderthals were just plain people, no more different from people living today than one living nation is different from another. What were the "cave men"? Just people who lived in caves. (And at today's housing prices, that may once again be a good idea!)

There's a secular museum in Germany where the curator dressed the wax model of a Neanderthal Man in a business suit and tie. His reason? He said it was time to quit deceiving the public. Neanderthals were just plain people. Indeed, scientists now classify Neanderthals as *Homo sapiens*, the same scientific name given to you and me.

Tragically, Neanderthals have not been the only people once considered subhuman "missing links." In an article reprinted in *Natural History* as part of an issue on the history of evolutionary thought, there's a short but very sad article by Henry Fairfield Osborn.[17] Osborn says that a hypothetical unbiased zoologist from Mars would classify people into several distinct genera and many species. Thus, said Osborn, Negroes would be classified as a separate species, not yet evolved to full human stature. "The standard of intelligence of the average adult Negro," wrote Osborn as a so-called fact of evolution, "is similar to that of the eleven-year-old youth of the species *Homo sapiens* [which, for Osborn, meant Caucasians only]." Osborn was a leading evolutionist of the 1920's, and it is easy to see how his kind of evolutionary thinking (rejected by modern evolutionists) helped to pave the way for Hitler's Nazi racism in the '30's and '40's. (See also Gould, on the false science of "craniometry" and its terrible applications.[18])

The Australian Aborigines were also once treated as subhuman evolutionary links. The natives of Tasmania were deliberately slaughtered by settlers who justified themselves by saying it was okay to kill wild dogs as farm pests, so why not other non-humans? As her dying wish, the last surviving Tasmanian, Truganini, asked that she be buried with her "people," not embalmed as a museum specimen. She died, was embalmed, and preserved as an evolutionary link. (Warning: few Christians stood against this horror, perhaps because many churches had already accepted evolution into their thinking.)

In 1912, speculation about man's ancestry shifted to Piltdown Man, dignified by the scientific name *Eoanthropus dawsoni*. Almost everyone knows that Piltdown Man turned out to be a deliberate hoax. But Piltdown Man wasn't shown to be a hoax until the 1950's. For over 40 years, the subtle message of the textbooks was clear: You can believe in creation if you want to, but the facts are all on the side of evolution. The *facts*, in this case, turned out to be a bit of ape jaw and human skull stained to make them look older.

One mystery is, who perpetrated the Piltdown hoax, but the real mystery is *why did anyone believe it*? It was *not* a particularly clever hoax. As Gould[19] points out, when people looked at the teeth with the right hypothesis in mind, "the evidences of artificial abrasion [filing] immediately sprang to the eye. Indeed so obvious did they seem it may well be asked—how was it that they had escaped notice before?" The age-stain was better done, but the imported mammalian fossils and hand-crafted tools were again obvious frauds. People *wanted* to believe in evolution, so they were able to see what they *wanted to believe* (a "people problem" that can only be solved by honestly looking at alternate sides of an issue).

Sometimes people ask me how virtually all the evolutionists in the world could be so wrong about such an important issue as human origins. Answer: it wouldn't be the first time. Science is a human endeavor, and human beings make mistakes. Evolution goes far beyond the limits of science, and is even more easily influenced by human bias. *I* know that both intellectually and personally since *I* once accepted the evolutionary bias and its view of the evidence.

The "human factor" in the study of human origins is apparent in the multiple and varied interpretations of Java and Peking Man ("*Homo erectus*") recounted in a very readable, yet thoroughly documented, new book by Marvin Lubenow, *Bones of Contention*.[20]

Joining Neanderthals, Blacks, Aborigines, and Piltdown Man as proposed witnesses for human evolution at the famous Scopes trial in 1925 was Nebraska Man. Nebraska Man was dignified by the scientific name *Hesperopithecus haroldcookii*, but he was never known by anything but a tooth. By imagination, the tooth was put in a skull, the skull was put on a skeleton, and the skeleton was given flesh, hair, and a family! Fig. 28 includes a picture of Nebraska Man redrawn from a London newspaper published during the year of the Scopes trial.

Two years later, Nebraska Man was back to being just a tooth. The tooth was found in the real skull, attached to the real skeleton. It turned out not to be the tooth of man's ape-like ancestor, but the tooth of an extinct pig!

A. *Neanderthals* turned out to be just plain people, some of whom suffered from bone diseases. In proper attire, they would attract no particular attention today.

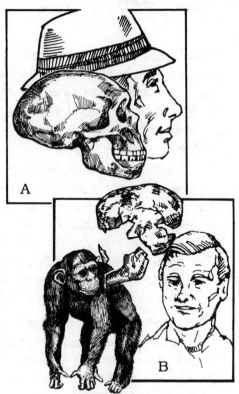

B. *Piltdown Man* (*Eoanthropus dawsoni*) was a deliberate (but not very clever) hoax palmed off as "proof of evolution" to students for more than two generations. It turned out to be a bit of ape jaw and human skull artificially aged.

C. *Nebraska Man* (*Hesperopithecus*) was reconstructed, family and all, from a tooth—a tooth that later was found to belong to an extinct pig!

Figure 28. Discarded candidates for man's ancestor.

Most evolutionists have long since learned not to make so much of a tooth. Yet it was not until 1979 that *Ramapithecus*—"reconstructed as a biped on the basis of teeth and jaws alone"—was dropped as a "false start of the human parade" (Zihlman and Lowenstein[21]). That didn't stop Elwyn Simons[22] from suggesting that *Aegyptopithecus* is a "nasty little thing" whose social behavior and family life—conjured up largely from eye sockets and the canine teeth of the males—are supposed to make it a kind of psychological ancestor of man!

The Australian National Museum in Sidney has apparently found a solution to the problem of evolutionary links still missing between apes and man. In June of 1993, we were greeted by a display describing five kinds of apes: lemurs, orangs, gorillas, chimps, and man. No need to look for links between apes and mankind if human beings are *still* apes! One display, described nursing behavior in various apes, including people. Another showed that man and chimps are the only apes that murder their own kind. A third pictured love-making among people and other apes. The text mentioned that some apes were monogamous, others polygamous or promiscuous, and that some men were like gorillas, others like chimps, etc. It was a truly inspiring and edifying display! Most evolutionists, of course, would be just as disgusted by the displays as would anyone else with a respect for science (or for common sense).

Modern speculation on mankind's ancestry centers on a group of fossils called *Australopithecus*. In the public mind, these fossils are associated especially with the work in Africa of the Leakey family and of Donald Johanson and his famous specimen, "Lucy" (Fig. 29).

The name *Australopithecus* means "southern ape," and it seems that apes are just what they are. Johanson likes to point out that where he finds his australopithecine bones, he finds many of the regular African animals (rhinos, boas, hippos, monkeys, etc.), but never apes. Could it be that apes are exactly what he has been finding all along? Its features are clearly ape-like—except that some claim Lucy and other australopithecines walked upright.

But how crucial to the definition of man is relatively upright posture? Vincent Sarich at the University of California in Berkeley and Adrienne Zihlman say that if you want something that walks upright, consider the living pygmy chimpanzee, *Pan paniscus*. This rare, rain-forest chimpanzee is only slightly shorter than the average chimpanzee, but it spends a fair amount of time walking upright. (I've watched them in the San Diego Zoo.) Since all the other features of the australopithecines are so apelike, perhaps Johanson and the Leakeys have discovered the ancestor of the living pygmy chimpanzee!

But did the australopithecines indeed walk upright? In the *American Biology Teacher*, Charles Oxnard[23] says:

> In one sense you may think there is no problem. For most anthropologists are agreed that the gracile australopithecines ... are on the main human lineage .... This is the view that is presented in almost all textbooks; I expect that it has been your teaching in the classroom; and it is widely broadcast in such publications as the "Time-Life Series" and the beautiful [television] story of "The Ascent of Man." However, anatomical features in some of these fossils provide a warning against a too-ready acceptance of this story. ...

As part of his warning, Oxnard reminds his readers of gross errors once made in the cases of Piltdown Man and Nebraska Man.

Oxnard then proceeds to examine the evidence. And he's well qualified to do so as Professor of Anatomy at the University of Southern California. He points out first that anatomical relationships cannot be simply established by subjective opinion. Viewed one way, for example, the pelvic bones of australopithecines seem to be intermediate between man and ape. But merely viewing the bones from a different angle makes the specimen seem as far distant from man as the other apes are. "Yet another view," says Oxnard, "might suggest that the fossil arose from the African apes via modern humans!"—in other words, that *humans* were the missing link between the apes and the australopithecines!

Because he is so sensitive to the serious problems of subjective interpretations, Oxnard then goes on to describe in fascinating detail a computer technique called "multivariate analysis." He goes into both its practical and its theoretic applications and reaches two conclusions.

First, his scientific conclusion: if the australopithecines walked upright, it was *not* in the human manner. If their posture resembled that of any living creature, it was most likely the orangutan. Oxnard also reaches a second conclusion for educators: "*Be critical.*" That is, examine all the relevant evidence. Look at it from different viewpoints. That's really the only way we can protect ourselves against bias in science or any other human endeavor: a willingness to constantly check assumptions and to listen respectfully to the views of others. I trust that's what we're doing in this book, and I wish students around the world had the same freedom to explore both sides of the creation-evolution issue.

Louis Leakey started the modern interest in australopithecines (and captured the attention of *National Geographic*) way back in 1959 with his "ape man," *Zinjanthropus. Zinjanthropus* has since been reclassified as *Austalopithecus bosei*, and it is now considered grossly apelike, an extinct ape really not related to man at all.

In fact, it was not the skeletal features that attracted attention to the Leakey finds in the first place. It was tools. As I said at the beginning of this book, every scientist can recognize

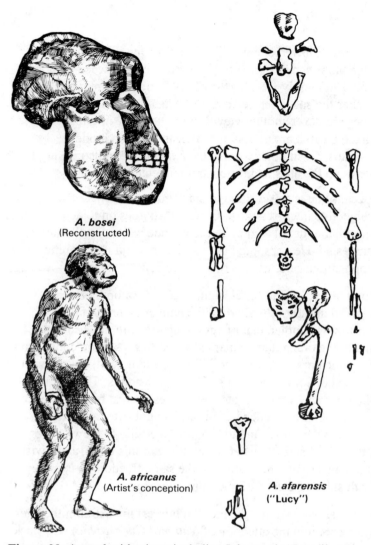

A. bosei
(Reconstructed)

A. africanus
(Artist's conception)

A. afarensis
("Lucy")

Figure 29. Australopithecines, including Johanson's "Lucy" and the Leakey finds in Africa, are the current candidates for man's ancestors. But USC's Charles Oxnard says the fossils "provide a warning against too ready acceptance of this view." He reaches two conclusions. One is scientific: "If the australopithecines walked upright, it was not in the human manner." The second is educational: "Be critical." We must encourage our science students to examine evidence more critically, he says—and, I might add, that's what the two-model creation-evolution concept is all about.

evidence of creation. Tools imply a tool maker. Since the tools were found with *Australopithecus*, Louis Leakey assumed that that creature had made the tools. Thirteen years later, Richard Leakey found beneath the bones his father had unearthed "bones virtually indistinguishable from those of modern man." Perhaps that solved the tool-maker mystery. At the time, Richard Leakey said his discovery shattered standard beliefs in evolution.

Actually, fossil discoveries have been *shattering* standard beliefs in evolution with monotonous regularity. Each in its day was hailed as "scientific proof" that human beings evolved from apelike animals, yet all the candidates once proposed as our evolutionary ancestors have been knocked off the list. The cover story in *Time* magazine for March 14, 1994, *assumes* that evolution is an absolute fact,[24] but it summarizes what is really the evaporating case for human evolution with these dramatic words:

> Yet despite more than a century of digging, the fossil record remains *maddeningly sparse*. With so few clues, even *a single bone* that doesn't fit into the picture *can upset everything*. Virtually every major discovery has put *deep cracks* in the conventional wisdom and forced scientists to *concoct new theories*, amid furious debate.[Empahsis added.]

It's sad that human evolution is still taught as "fact" to school children, college students, and the general public, when "virtually every major discovery" has discredited the so-called evidence and disproved the theory. Even sadder, scientists who know the evidence and are "forced to concoct new theories" are only concocting new theories of *how* human evolution occurred, unwilling to ask *whether* evolution occurred and to work on the truly new, non-evolutionary theories that the evidence demands.

The australopithecines could not have been our ancestors, of course, if *people* were walking around *before* Lucy and her kin were fossilized—and there is evidence to suggest just that. Fossils of ordinary people in mid-Tertiary rock were found in Castenidolo, Italy, back in the late 1800's, and the evolutionist Sir Arthur Keith recognized that accepting these "pre-ape" finds would shatter his belief in evolution (or at least its scientific support). Oxnard[25] and Lubenow[26] call attention to the *Kanapoi hominid*, a human upper arm bone found in rock strata in Africa laid down *before* those that entomb the australopithecine remains.

Then there's the footprint evidence. Actually, we have many features in common with the apes (as a trip to the zoo will verify), and it should not be surprising that some bones would be difficult to classify. But apes and human beings have quite different footprints. The apes have essentially "four hands," with an opposable big toe that makes their footprint quite different from ours. They also have a gait that's quite different and a tendency to drop to all fours and "knuckle walk."

In *National Geographic*[27] and *Science News*,[28] Mary Leakey describes a trail of man-like prints in volcanic ash near Laetoli in east Africa. Fig. 30, redrawn from the former, shows Mary Leakey's concept of how the prints were formed and preserved and the kind of foot that made them. If you examine the article, you'll find that the foot looks pretty much like yours or mine.

In the center of the *National Geographic* article is a two-page fold out. Elephants, giraffes, guinea hens, and acacia trees dot the scene. Except for the volcano, it looks as if it could have been taken from a Tarzan movie. Then across the center is a line of very human-like tracks. You might be surprised, however, at what the artist put *in* the tracks. An artist had to do it, by the way, since we have no foot bones connected to leg bones, etc., to tell us what really made the tracks. Perhaps the most logical inference from these observations is that

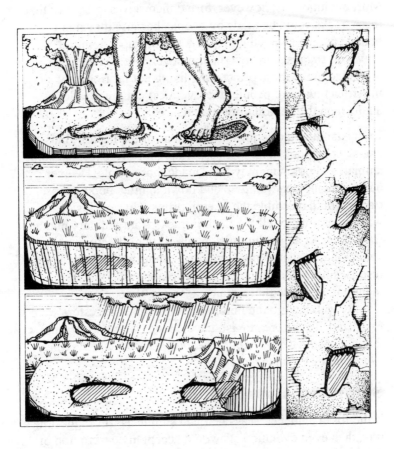

Figure 30. Footprints are more distinctive of man than most bone fragments are. If the footprints above are accepted as human, evolutionists would have to say that man existed "before" man's supposed ancestors. Creationists say that these footprints (and the Castenedolo and Kanapoi bones) simply suggest that people have always been people, beginning with the first created human beings.

people made them. The stride is quite short, but perhaps the person was small or just very cautious about walking across the damp volcanic ash.

Most evolutionists, however, forbid themselves to believe that these tracks could be made by people, because they don't believe people evolved until later. The Kanapoi hominid, however, suggests that people might very well have been around to make these prints. And living not far from that site in Africa today are people (the Pygmies) not much taller as adults than the Laetoli print-makers.

Understanding the serious implications of the Laetoli finds, one scientist looked almost desperately for evidence that some animal, and not man, may have made those prints. He even had a dancing bear jump up and down in mud, hoping those tracks would resemble the Laetoli prints! His conclusion? It was impossible to tell the Laetoli tracks from ordinary human footprints. As an evolutionist, he used such adjectives as "shocking," "disturbing," and "upsetting" to describe his results, since none of the popular evolutionary "links," including Lucy, could be man's ancestor, if people were already walking around before these so-called ancestors were fossilized. To the creationist, the evidence simply confirms that *people have always been people, and apes always apes, as far back as the evidence goes.*

Summary: Fossil Kinds

If the fossil evidence is as clear and simple as I'm suggesting it is, then even evolutionists would accept my description of the facts (even if they violently disagreed with my Biblical inferences), and they do. Leading evolutionists from around the world met for a major conference in Chicago in 1980. In chapter two, we discussed the "genetic conclusions" reached at that conference. Evolutionists at the Chicago conference also reached some remarkable conclusions about fossils.[29,30] Without giving creationists any credit, the world's leading evolutionists at that Chicago conference at least agreed on the same assessment of the fossil evidence reached (and predicted) by creationists long ago. As the summary in *Newsweek* put it (emphasis added):

> ***Evidence from fossils now points overwhelmingly away from the classical Darwinism which most Americans learned in high school.***

In building up to that monumental conclusion (which should be posted as a plaque in all the nation's science classrooms), the writer starts with man (emphasis added):

> The missing link between man and the apes . . . is merely the most glamorous of a whole hierarchy of *phantom creatures.* In the fossil record, *missing links are the rule. . . . The more scientists have searched for the transitional forms between species, the more they have been frustrated.*

The concept of evolution touted in textbooks, then, is based on phantoms and figments of the imagination, *not* on fossils and the facts of science. Stephen Gould and Niles Eldredge[31] put it this way: "Phyletic gradualism [gradual evolution] . . . was never 'seen' in the rocks." *Evolution was never seen in the rocks*! Evolution is *not* a logical inference from scientific observations, because the observations were contrary to the theory right from the start, even as Darwin said.

If it wasn't based on evidence or logic, then, where did the concept of evolution come from? Gould and Eldredge supply the answer: "It [gradual evolution] expressed the cultural and political biases of 19th century liberalism." That's what has been passed off in our school systems for 100 years as the "fact of evolution"—"*the cultural and political biases of 19th century liberalism.*"

When it comes to the fossil evidence, what are the facts? Believe it or not, when it comes to fossils, *evolutionists and creationists now agree on what the facts are*. The overwhelming pattern that emerges from fossils we have found is summarized in the word *stasis*. *Stasis* and *static* come from the same root word, a word that means "stay the same." Gould and Eldredge are simply saying that most kinds of fossilized life forms appear in the fossil sequence abruptly and distinctly as discrete kinds, then show relatively minor variation within kind, and finally abruptly disappear.

Steven Stanley,[32] fossil expert from Johns Hopkins University, provides several examples of stasis. Elephants (*Primelephas*) appear as a distinct group abruptly in the fossil sequence, diversify immediately into three subtypes, which then persist unchanged (except those which became extinct) without noticeably changing into anything else. Similarly, the modern horses (*Equus*) appear abruptly, Stanley says, "and their origin is not documented by known fossil evidence." Stanley also notes that the excellent fossil history of bowfin fishes shows only trivial changes, and no basic shift of adaptation, making them very much like their descendants.

Stanley fully intends for the concept of stasis—sudden distinct appearance, minor variation, sudden disappearance—to stand out in stark contrast to the popular textbook and television picture of gradual, mutation-selection evolution. He singles out particularly the oft-taught "fact" of mammalian adaptive radiation, the idea that a mouse-like animal (without a mouse's gnawing front teeth) evolved into swimming whales and flying bats and all the other mammal types within about 12 million years. Trying to explain that on the basis of slow selection of minor mutational changes that would need a million years to transform just one species, he says, *"is clearly preposterous"* (emphasis added). Creationists only wish that evolutionists like Stanley were around decades ago, when creationists were pointing to the evidence, both genetic and fossil, that seemed even back then to make such an idea *"clearly preposterous!"*

The victory of stasis over gradualism did not come easily at the Chicago conference. As Lewin[33] mentioned in his summary for *Science*, "the proceedings were at times unruly and even acrimonious," but, on the positive side, "many people suggested that the meeting was a turning point in the history of evolutionary thought."

Perhaps the most dramatic response came from Francisco Ayala. After admitting that neo-Darwinists "would not have predicted stasis from population genetics [extrapolation from mutation and selection]," he concluded, "but I am now convinced from what the paleontologists say that *small changes do not accumulate.*" (Emphasis added.) No one finds it easy to change years of thinking, but a willingness to adapt theory to fact is the mark of a true scientist, and Ayala deserves a lot of credit for his statement.

When the dust finally settled, Gabriel Dover of Cambridge University summarized the Chicago conference by calling species stasis "the single most important feature of macroevolution." Note, again, that at least the creationists and evolutionists agree on what the fossil facts represent, namely, **stasis**: *sudden appearance of complete forms, minor variation, and sudden disappearance.*

But perhaps you also detected a note of irony in Dover's comment. If stasis means anything, it means staying the same; if evolution means anything, it means change. It seems to me, then, that evolutionists are actually saying (without quite meaning to, of course) that *the most fundamental fact of their theory of change is that everything stays the same*!

Creationists prefer a much more direct approach to the evidence. Each basic kind of plant and animal life appears in the fossil sequence *complete, fully formed*, and *functional*; each classifies according to the criteria we use to distinguish groups today, with "boundary problems" generally no greater nor different for extinct forms than for those living today; and each kind shows broad but quite finite ecologic and geographic variation within its kind. The most direct and logical inference (to a heart and mind open to the possibility) appears to be, it seems to me, *creation, and variation within the basic created kinds*. Differences such as extinction and decline in size and variety seem to point to the *corruption* and *catastrophe* in the created order, not at all to "upward, onward" evolution.

When Darwin published *Origin* back in 1859, no one knew what discoveries would be made or what patterns would emerge in the new science of paleontology. On the basis of their theory and the observations of heredity and reproduction, creationists predicted that only distinct kinds would be found, variation only within kind, and persistence of the criteria for classification. Evolutionists predicted a series of links would be found to show how complex types today evolved slowly and gradually from common ancestral stocks that finally blurred into simple, indistinct, and difficult-to-classify early forms.

The real test of a scientific theory is its ability to predict in advance of observation. When it comes to fossils, *creation has passed the scientific test with flying colors*. The original Darwinian theory of evolution and the neo-Darwinist and punctuationalist views, have been disproven twice, both by genetics and by the fossil evidence.

In his final chapter, as he reviews his reasons for calling his book *Evolution: A Theory in Crisis,* Denton[34] makes the following strong, sometimes harsh, statements:

> We now know, as a result of discoveries made over the past thirty years, that not only is there a distinct break between the animate [living] and inanimate [non-living] worlds, but that it is one of the most dramatic in all nature, absolutely *unbridged by any series of transitional forms* ["missing links"], and like so many other major gaps of nature, *the transitional forms are not only*

empirically absent but are also conceptually impossible [p. 347, emphasis added].

Similarly, the sorts of scenarios conjured up by evolutionary biologists to bridge the great divisions of nature, *those strange realms of "pro-avis" or the "proto-cell" which are so utterly unrealistic to the skeptic*, are often viewed by the believers [in evolution] as further powerful confirmatory evidence of the truth of the paradigm. Evolutionary thought today provides many other instances where the priority of the paradigm [i.e., the assumption that "evolution is fact"] takes precedence over common sense [p. 352, emphasis added].

For the skeptic or indeed to anyone prepared to step out of the circle of Darwinian belief, it is not hard to find inversions of common sense in modern evolutionary thought which are strikingly reminiscent of the mental gymnastics of the phlogiston chemists or the medieval astronomers (p. 351).

In a very real sense, therefore, advocacy of the doctrine of continuity [i.e., evolutionism] has always necessitated a retreat from pure empiricism [i.e., logic and observation], and contrary to what is widely assumed by evolutionary biologists today, *it has always been the anti-evolutionists* [i.e., creationists], *not the evolutionists, in the scientific community who have stuck rigidly to the facts and adhered to a more strictly empirical approach. . . . It was Darwin the evolutionist who was retreating from the facts* [pp. 353–354 emphasis added].

On the positive side, Denton also notes that "there has always existed a significant minority of first-rate biologists who have never been able to bring themselves to accept the validity of Darwinian claims" (p. 327). At a conference in Sydney, Australia (April, 1987), where we appeared on the platform together, Denton was willing to cautiously extrapolate that "significant minority" to "perhaps a majority" of first-rate biologists. And he stresses also that those biologists willing to explore the design hypothesis do so for scientific reasons, apart from particular religious presuppositions, (p. 341).

Creation-evolution was featured on CBS television "Sunday Morning" (Nov. 23, 1980) in a superb cover story put together by Richard Threlkeld[35] (who ranks up there with CBC's Tom Kelly as a fair, honest, thoughtful, and thought-provoking TV journalist). The 20-minute piece starts with my students and me "in the act of discovery," hunting fossils in the desert east of San Diego. It continues with several evolutionists, other creationists, parents, students, and teachers in action; and it concludes with my favorite evolutionist, Stephen J. Gould, and with a clip from Carl Sagan's *Cosmos* TV series.

Threlkeld makes the inevitable trip to the site of the famous Scopes "monkey trial," but he does not allow his thinking to be buried there. "The debate goes on," he observes, "and why not?" After all, nobody was there to see how life came into being, he says; at bottom both views are assumptions. But he doesn't stop thinking there, either. Instead, he treats the two ultimate assumptions, creation and evolution, as ideas which *can* be compared for their scientific merits and which *must* be compared before we can truly appreciate our origin as human beings.

II. HOW FAST?

All the courses I took concerning fossils were taught by professors who firmly believed in evolution. Yet, when it came to the kinds of life we studied, it seemed the actual evidence made it overwhelmingly difficult to believe in evolution and very easy to believe what the Bible says about Creation, Corruption, Catastrophe, and Christ.

But even if you could accept my conclusion, or, at least, consider it reasonable, I'm sure you'd have another question:

How fast do fossils form, and *how fast* do rock layers get stacked up like we see in Grand Canyon? Believe me, those questions bothered me, too! I knew that some believed, for example, that even though God especially created the first of each kind, he "spaced out" His creative activity over a vast period of time, a sort of "progressive creation."

Can science help us decide how fast fossils form, and how fast those sedimentary rock layers pile up? That's what I wanted to know when I signed up for courses like Stratigraphy that deal in part with rates of sediment-layer formation.

Surprisingly enough, just about everybody—creationist, evolutionist, and everyone in between—agrees that individual fossil specimens themselves begin to form very, very rapidly! If a plant or animal just dies and falls to the ground or into the water, it's quickly broken up and decomposed by scavengers, wind and water currents, even sunlight. Fallen logs, road kills, and dead aquarium fish don't just become fossils, nor did the millions of bison slaughtered in America's move west.

Most fossils are formed when a plant or animal is quickly and deeply buried, out of reach of scavengers and currents, usually in mud, lime, or sand sediment rich in cementing minerals that harden and preserve at least parts of the dead creatures. Evolutionists and creationists agree: the ideal conditions for forming most fossils and fossil-bearing rock layers are *flood conditions*. The debate is just whether it was many "little floods" over a long time, or mostly the one big Flood of Noah's time. In fact, until Darwin's theory came along, most educated laymen and scientists—including the founding fathers of geology—assumed that fossils were the remains of plants and animals buried in Noah's Flood.

Although professionals understand how fast fossils begin to form under flood conditions, the general public often does not. I was on a radio talk show one time when a caller said he believed the earth had to be fantastically old because he'd seen (as I have) huge logs turned to stone in Arizona's Petrified Forest. Surely, he said, it would take millions of years to turn a log six feet (2m) across into solid stone! So I asked him to think about it. If a tree fell over in a forest or into a lake or stream and just lay there for millions of years, wouldn't it just rot away? Bugs, termites, fungus, chemical action would soon turn it back into dust. But *if* that tree got suddenly and deeply buried in mineral-rich sediment, *then* minerals could crystallize throughout the log and turn it to stone before it had time to decay. To my encouragement, he replied, "You know, I believe you're right about that!"

A museum in central Tasmania has a "fossil hat" on display. A miner had dropped his felt hat, and, the limey water had turned it into a "hard hat" (which the curator was kind enough to let me feel and photograph). That same process, mineral in-fill, can turn wood, bones, and shells into fossils in a short period of time. Indeed, fossils can be made in the laboratory!

Remember the Precambrian Australian jellyfish? Jellyfish often wash ashore, but in a matter of hours they have turned into nondescript "blobs" (although watch out—the stinging cells continue to work for quite a while!) To preserve the markings and detail of the Ediacara jellyfish, the organisms seem to have landed on a wet sand that acted as a natural cement. The sand turned to sandstone before the jellyfish had time to rot, preserving the jellyfish's markings, somewhat as you can preserve your hand print if you push it into cement during that brief time when it's neither too wet nor too dry. Indeed, the evolutionist who discovered the Ediacara jellyfish said the fossils must have formed in *less than 24 hours*. He didn't mean one jellyfish in 24 hours; he meant millions of jellyfish and other forms had fossilized throughout the entire Ediacara formation, which stretches about 300 miles or 500 km from South Australia into the Northern Territory, in less than 24 hours! In short, **floods form fossils fast!** (See Fig.31)

Like most Americans, I was mis-taught in grade school that it takes millions of years and tremendous heat and pressure to turn sediments (like sand, lime, or clay) into rock (like sandstone, limestone, or shale). We all know better. Concrete is just artificial rock. Cement companies crush rock, separate the cementing minerals and large stones, then sell it to you. You add water to produce the chemical reaction (curing, not drying), and rock forms again—easily, naturally, and quickly, right before your very eyes. Indeed, you can make rock as a geology lab exercise, without using volcanic heat and pressure or waiting millions of years for the results. Time, heat, and pressure can and do alter the *properties* of rock (including "Flood rock"), but the initial *formation* of most rocks, like the setting of concrete, is quite rapid.

There are many areas where hordes of large animals are entombed in a thick rock layer, such as the dinosaurs preserved along the Red Deer River in Alberta, Canada. Once a plant or animal is buried deeply enough in the right kind of sediment, there's no special trick involved in turning it into fossil, and no huge amount of time is required. Minerals simple accumulate in the specimen itself or in the cavity left by the specimen after it rots away. So, fossils can be formed in the laboratory, and they are probably forming here and there today.

But nowhere on earth today do we have fossils forming on the scale that we see in geologic deposits. The Karroo Beds in Africa, for example, contain the remains of perhaps 800 billion vertebrates! A million fish can be killed in red tides in the Gulf of Mexico today, but they simply decay away and do not become fossils. Similarly, debris from vegetation mats doesn't become coal unless it is buried under a heavy load of sediment.

Figure 31. Because massive flooding seems to be the most logical inference from our observations of fossil deposits, a number of evolutionary geologists are now calling themselves "neo-catastrophists." *Catastrophist geology*, originally a creationist idea associated with Noah's Flood, has stimulated a great deal of research, and it helps us to understand how fossils form (*above*) and why such huge numbers are spread over such broad areas (*below*).

Some geologic formations are spread out over vast areas of a whole continent. For example, there's the Morrison Formation, famous for its dinosaur remains, that covers much of the mountainous West, and there's the St. Peter's Sandstone, a glass sand that stretches from Canada to Texas and from the Rockies to the Appalachians. Sediment does build up slowly at the mouths of rivers, such as the Mississippi delta. But slow sediment build-up could not possibly produce such widespread deposits, such broadly consistent sedimentary and paleontological features, as we see in the Morrison and St. Peter's formations. In this case, knowledge of the present tells us that something happened on a much larger scale in the past than we see it happening anywhere today. That's not appealing to faith or fancy; that's appealing to fact! For purely scientific reasons, evolutionists and creationists may both conclude these are flood deposits, even if the scale of the flood is something far beyond anything observed in historical times.[36]

Knowledgeable people readily agree that both fossils and rock layers can and do form very rapidly. But there's a catch. Fossils and rock layers are *not* just found "one at a time." Rocks chock full of fossils are buried in layers stacked on top of one another, in places about *2 miles* (*3km*) *thick*! Not only that, but there's a tendency for fossils to be found together in certain groups, and a tendency for these groups to be found one after the other in a certain sequence called the "*geologic column.*"

According to evolution, the geologic column (Fig. 32) lays out the story of evolution chronologically, from bottom to top, right before our eyes. Maybe science hasn't explained how evolution works yet, but the "fact of evolution" is plain to see in the "record in the rocks." Life started with a few simple life forms (originally produced by time, chance, and chemistry), and we can chart its progress, the net increase in variety and complexity, as we move up through the rock layers. Only an ignorant, fundamentalist fanatic with his nose in the Bible could fail to see evidence so clear and convincing as the "rock-hard" geologic column!

Or at least that's the way textbooks, television, museums, and magazines usually tell the story, and that's the evolutionary story I used to teach, too. What is someone who believes the Bible going to say? There really are fossils out there; they really are in sedimentary rock layers; and those layers really are stacked on top of each other, over 1.5 miles (2 km) deep across the Arizona-Utah border, for example.

Now the geologic column is an *idea*, *not* an actual series of rock layers. Nowhere do we find the complete sequence. But, still, the geologic column *does* represent a tendency for fossils to be found in groups and for those groups to be found in a certain vertical order. Cambrian trilobites and Cretaceous dinosaurs aren't usually found together. I found the trilobite I wear as a bolo tie, for instance, in Madison, Indiana, but our family's collection of dinosaur bones came from Alberta, Canada.

Why aren't trilobite and dinosaur fossils found together? According to evolution, the answer is easy. The Cambrian trilobites died out millions of years before the dinosaurs evolved. But there is *another* explanation that seems even *more natural*. After all, even if trilobites and dinosaurs were alive today, they still wouldn't be found together. Why? Because they live in different ecological zones. Dinosaurs are land animals, but trilobites are bottom-dwelling sea creatures.

According to creationists, the geological systems represent different ecological zones, the buried remains of plants and animals that once lived together in the same environment. A walk through Grand Canyon, then, is not like a walk through evolutionary time; instead, it's like a walk from the bottom of the ocean, across the tidal zone, over the shore, across the lowlands, and into the upland regions. Several lines of evidence seem to favor *this ecological view*.

First, there's the matter of "misplaced fossils." Evolutionists believe, for example, that the land plants did not appear until over 100 million years after the Cambrian trilobites died out. Yet, over sixty genera of woody-plant spores, pollen, and wood itself have been recovered from lowest "trilobite rock" (Cambrian) throughout the world. The evidence is so well known that it's even in standard college biology textbooks. The secular botany textbook by Weier, Stocking, and Barbour[37] that my students once used puts it this way: "Despite tempting fragments of evidence, such as cutinized [waxy] spores and bits of xylem [wood] dating back to the Cambrian period . . . ," most evolutionists still believe that land plants did not evolve until much later. But notice, the evolutionist argues "in spite of the evidence."

The creationist does not argue *"in spite* of the evidence." Rather, *"because* of the evidence," the creationist says, "we think that land plants and Cambrian trilobites lived at the same time in different places. Normally, these sea animals and land plants would not be preserved together for ecological reasons. But a few plant specimens, escaping decay, could occasionally be entombed with trilobites in ocean sediment, and that's what we see."

Misplaced fossils are common enough that evolutionists have a vocabulary to deal with them. A specimen found "too low" in the geologic column (before it was *supposed* to have evolved) is called a "stratigraphic leak," and a specimen found "too high" is called a "re-worked specimen." Often, of course, there is actual physical evidence for mixing of strata from two different sources. But sometimes, such evidence is lacking. With such a handy vocabulary available, it's quite likely that the number of misplaced fossils found—without evidence of disturbance—is far greater than the number actually recorded (which is considerable anyway).

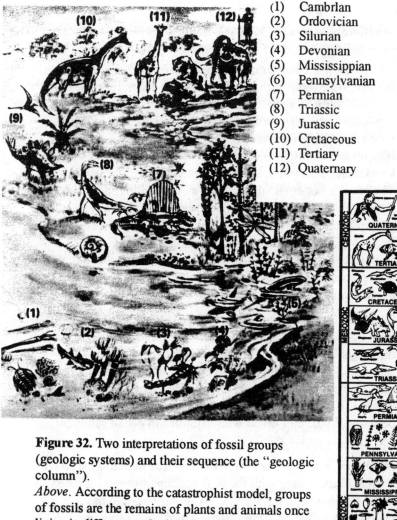

(1)	Cambrian
(2)	Ordovician
(3)	Silurian
(4)	Devonian
(5)	Mississippian
(6)	Pennsylvanian
(7)	Permian
(8)	Triassic
(9)	Jurassic
(10)	Cretaceous
(11)	Tertiary
(12)	Quaternary

Figure 32. Two interpretations of fossil groups (geologic systems) and their sequence (the "geologic column").

Above. According to the catastrophist model, groups of fossils are the remains of plants and animals once living in different ecological zones at the same time, and they were buried in rapid succession. (Drawings after Bliss, Parker, and Gish. 1980. *Fossils: Key to the Present.* Master Books, Colorado Springs)

Right. According to the uniformitarian model, systems and the geologic column represent stages in the slow and gradual evolution of life over aeons of time.

Sometimes whole geologic systems are misplaced. While I was a graduate student in stratigraphy class still trying to decide between the Bible and evolution, we went on a field trip to find the missing 25 million years of the Silurian. We went to a quarry in southern Indiana that was famous for building-quality limestone. The massive gray limestone was quite thick and exposed over many hundreds of yards. In the lower part of the formation, we found corals belonging to system No. 2, the Ordovician. But as we worked our way up the quarry wall, suddenly we began to find Devonian corals, those belonging to system No. 4. Where were the missing corals of system No. 3, the Silurian?

For an evolutionist, that's a crucial question. Evolutionists believe that Ordovician corals *evolved into* Silurian corals, which evolved into Devonian corals. Skipping the Silurian would break the evolutionary chain, and for an evolutionist would be impossible!

What was there between the Ordovician and Devonian corals in that limestone quarry in Indiana? Only millimeters separated them, and there was no change in color, no change in texture, not even a bedding plane. There was *no physical evidence at all* for those hypothetical 25 million years of evolutionary time. As the professor emphasized, such a situation is a serious problem for evolution. We simply can't imagine land just lying there for 25 million years, he said, neither eroding nor depositing, then picking up exactly where it left off!

Evolutionists have coined a term to deal with the problem: *paraconformity*. A contact line between two rock strata is called a "conformity" if the physical evidence indicates smooth continuous deposition with no time break. "Disconformity" is used where the physical evidence indicates erosion has removed part of the rock sequence. Disconformities are often represented by wavy lines in geologic diagrams, and they often appear in the field as *real* "wavy lines" in which erosion channels and stream beds can be seen cutting into the eroded rock layer. But in the case of a *paraconformity*, there is no evidence of erosion, nor any other physical evidence of a break in time, only fossils "out of place." The name even means that it *looks like* a conformity. In fact, the only way to recognize a paraconformity is by prior commitment to evolutionary theory. There is no physical evidence! But if you believe in evolution, then you must believe there was some gap in the sequence, or else the evolutionary chain would be broken.

Creationists don't need the term paraconformity. Creationists can simply accept the physical evidence as it's found: smooth, continuous deposition with no time break. Suppose the Ordovician and Devonian geologic systems represent different ecological zones of creatures living at the same time. Then a change in some ecological factor, such as saltiness or temperature, could cause one group of corals to replace the other ecologically, smoothly, and continuously. Or sediment from one ecological zone could be deposited immediately on top of sediment from another zone as currents changed direction, again producing smooth continuous deposition with no time break. I included an explanation like that in my answer to an exam question about paraconformities. I got an "A" on the essay (and on the test), and the professor was intrigued with the possibility—but said he couldn't accept it because of the time span involved.

Many people think that if Christians could only accept great age, they'd have no problem with science. Actually, they would have no problem with *evolution*, but lots of problems with *science*! Gould[38] laments that geologists are constantly reporting ecological interpretations of fossil deposits, but he says they should quit doing that, because the time scale is all wrong for evolution. Perhaps the ecological interpretations—based on actual physical evidence—are *correct*, and it's the evolutionary time scale—based on faith in evolution—that's *wrong*! Belief in great age and slow change make it very difficult to understand many physical features of our earth.

Consider *polystratic* fossils. As the name implies, polystrates are fossils that extend through many rock layers or strata. I first heard of polystratic fossils as a geology student. The professor, an evolutionist, was talking about zoning rocks on the basis of the microscopic fossils they contain. The usual assumption, of course, is that one microfossil evolved into another, which evolved into another, and so on. The rock unit he zoned was presumed to involve about 20 million years of evolutionary time. But then the professor told us he followed the rock unit down the creek bed, and found a shellfish, with a shell shaped like an ice cream cone, perched on its tip through the whole 20 million years! How could that be, he wondered. It couldn't perch on its tip for 20 million years waiting for sediment to accumulate, and it couldn't stab itself down through rock hardened over that time.

Polystrates are indeed a mystery for an evolutionist! But they would be no mystery at all, if the whole rock unit were deposited rapidly. Some things, like trees washed out in vegetation mats after a tropical storm, may float upright for a while, and they could be entombed in that upright position if burial occurred quickly enough (Fig. 33).

Polystrates are especially common in coal formations. For years and years, students have been taught that coal represents the remains of swamp plants slowly accumulated as peat and then even more slowly changed into coal. But there are many reasons that this swamp-idea simply cannot be true: the type of plants involved, texture of deposits, and state of preservation are all wrong; the action of flowing water, not stagnation, is evident.[39]

A new concept of coal formation is being developed right now, thanks in part to the work of creationist geologists. One

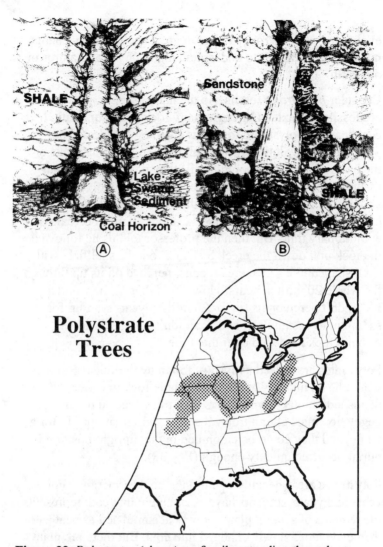

Polystrate
Trees

Figure 33. *Polystrates (above)* are fossils extending through "thousands or even millions of years" of hypothetical evolutionary time. Polystrates are especially common in coal. Because coal deposits extend over such broad areas (*right*), a growing number of geologists (evolutionists and creationists) think that coal must have been deposited rapidly under floating mats of plants ripped up in large-scale flood catastrophes.

of the leaders in this field is Dr. Steven Austin. In his dissertation for the Ph.D. in coal geology from Penn State, Dr. Austin[40] suggests that coal was formed from plant debris deposited under mats of vegetation floating in sea water. His model already explains many features of coal that the swamp-model cannot explain. Even more importantly, his theory—a real scientific breakthrough—is the first ever to be used to *predict* the location and quality of coal.

Dramatic confirmation of the processes postulated by Dr. Austin was provided by the eruption of Mt. St. Helens. The volcano sent mud and debris hurtling down into Spirit Lake, sloshing a wave nearly 900 feet (300 m) up its initially tree-studded slopes. The wave sheared off trees with enough lumber to make all the houses in a large city! The trees were sheared off their roots and stripped of their leaves, branches, and bark. The "forest" of denuded logs floated out over the huge lake. As they water-logged, many sank vertically down into and through several layers of mud on the lake bottom. Many features of the lake-bottom deposits are reminiscent of coal deposits. A fantastic video describing both the eruption of Mt. St. Helens and his original research has been prepared by Dr. Austin[41] and ought to be seen!

On a small scale, you can see the process that may have started the formation of coal deposits when a typhoon rips up mats of vegetation and floats them out to sea. But some coal seams run from Pennsylvania out across Ohio, Indiana, and Illinois into Iowa and down to Oklahoma! What kind of storm could be involved in the formation of that kind of coal seam? Answer: Catastrophic flooding on a scale like that described in the Bible for Noah's Flood!

Neo-Catastrophism

Catastrophism has always been an important part of creationist geology. In the 1800's, due especially to the influence of James Hutton and Charles Lyell, emphasis shifted to the concept of slow, gradual accumulation of sediments, a concept called uniformitarianism.[42] As Stephen Gould,[43] who teaches the history of science at Harvard, points out, this new idea was accepted largely on the basis of philosophic preference (i.e., "faith"). Although Gould is an anti-creationist, he says: "*Catastrophists* were as committed to science as any gradualist; in fact, *they adopted the more 'objective' view that one should believe what one sees* and not interpolate missing bits of gradual record into a literal tale of rapid change." (Emphasis added.)

Because of the objective evidence, a new group of evolutionary geologists has arisen. They call themselves "*neo-catastrophists*." Derek Ager,[44] past president of the British Geologic Association, says, " I have already declared myself an unrepentant 'neo-catastrophist.' " He goes on to say that the geologic evidence reminds him of the life of a soldier, full of "long periods of boredom and short periods of terror." It seems to me that the "long periods of boredom" are the contact lines between the strata (the *absence* of deposits where, *presumably*, all the evolution has occurred). The "short periods of terror" formed the fossil-bearing deposits themselves. It is rapid, large-scale processes that form the fossil-bearing deposits we actually observe.

Ager also interprets differences in geological formations as a result of "ecological expropriations," a rapid process involving replacement of one existing kind by another, i.e., ecology *not* evolution. Ager knows that the creationists are going to make use of his work, and he's absolutely right. We're not arguing our case on the strength of his opinion, however, but on the *evidence* that he knows so well. The evidence suggests rapid deposition on a large scale: *catastrophism*.

Scuba diving along Australia's Barrier Reef, I was startled and thrilled to find living crinoids ("sea lilies" or "feather stars"), sort of "upside-down starfish on stems." These graceful creatures (looking like plants, except that they can walk on their "roots"!) were once so abundant that the Mississippian System (Lower Carboniferous) is sometimes called the "Age (Zone) of Crinoids." I had found their fabulous fossils in Indiana, Iowa, and Nebraska, but evolutionary teaching had assured me this great group was an evolutionary dead end, unfit to survive except in a few out-of-the-way places! How stunningly untrue! Here were dozens, in a variety of brilliant colors, alive and doing very well in the richest (and most competitive) life zone on earth!

Forms like these feather stars that were once abundant but now extinct, or nearly so, are called "living fossils." Lampshells (brachiopods) are called "living fossils" because only a few genera survive of a group once so abundant they are sometimes called "fossil weeds." The "oldest" continuously surviving animal (the one with the longest stratigraphic range) is the lampshell called *Lingula*, which, in an evolutionary sense, might be considered the world's most successful animal, remaining completely unchanged while trilobites, dinosaurs, saber-tooth tigers, and other great creatures came and went around it!

The pearly *Nautilus* is called a living fossil because most members of its group, the squid-like cephalopod mollusks, have been eliminated by extinction. But why would evolution "do in" the nautiloids, the most complex (i.e., "most highly evolved") of all invertebrates, especially since the "first" nautiloids continue complete and complex—and unchanged, from the "beginning" of fossil abundance (lowest Cambrian rock)?

While it was known only from a few fossil bones presumed to be millions of years old, the coelacanth (*Latimeria*) was hailed as a "missing link," an animal caught in the act of evolving from fish to amphibian. But then they found coelacanths alive and well ("living fossils") off Madagascar—100% fish in a totally deep-sea-fish environment, the end of this "fish story" as *Scientific American* once called it. As regularly happens, additional evidence disproved, rather than supported, evolutionary belief. (Joachin Scheven,[45] one of Europe's leading creation scientists, has a museum with spectacular displays of these and many other "living fossils.")

Evolutionists have always been perplexed by "living fossils." These creatures are clearly well-fit to survive; they were complete and complex from their first appearance; and they have remained unchanged throughout vast stretches of *presumed* evolutionary time.

Catastrophism helps us to understand the patterns of extinction we see when we compare living forms with their fossil relatives. A catastrophe would wipe out creatures regardless of their environmental fitness. Only those that happen to be in the right place at the right time when the catastrophe hit would survive. David Raup,[46] well-known evolutionist, talks about this as "survival of the luckiest" in contrast to "survival of the fittest" (natural selection).

"Survival of the luckiest" would explain why present forms appear to be no more fit to survive than their fossil relatives. At best, only a few of each kind would survive, and these would possess less of the original created gene pool. Population-genetics textbooks even refer to these consequences of a "genetic bottleneck" as the "Noah's Ark Effect." That would help to explain why most groups existed in greater variety in times past than they do now—the *opposite* of evolutionary expectations, a reflection instead of the Biblical sequence: Creation, Corruption, Catastrophe.

Giant forms seem to have been particularly hard hit by extinction. As fossils, we find giant dragonflies with wingspans over 2 feet (60 cm); giant fusilinids among the one-celled creatures (½ inch (12 mm)is giant for them); the giant reptiles, including some of the dinosaurs; even a giant beaver that reached six feet (2 m) in body length. (Imagine looking up into the face of a giant beaver. When he says, "I want that tree," you respond, "Take it. It's yours!") Perhaps the giant beavers were for cutting down the giant trees. As I mentioned earlier, plants such as the club mosses or ground pines (lycopods), which grow only a few inches (centimeters) tall today, are represented as fossils (with the same kind of stem and "leaf" anatomy and reproductive structures) by trees reaching 120 feet (35 m) in height (the lepidodendrons).

Thanks to the eruption of Mt. St. Helens, scientists have had a chance to observe, measure, and study catastrophic processes close up.[47] The energy of the initial eruption was equivalent to that released by many atomic bombs. It blew off the top 1300 feet (ca. 400 m) of the mountain; produced a hot-blast cloud of 400°C moving at over 100 miles per hour (160 km/hr); generated mud flows tens of feet (several meters) thick, moving at 30 miles per hour (50 km/hr); and, as mentioned before, sheared off trees sufficient to build houses for an entire metropolitan area. My wife and I had the opportunity to fly up Mt. St. Helens, down into the crater, and out over the denuded mountainside and log jam in Spirit Lake—still awesome ten years after the first eruption. Yet, Mt. St. Helens was a "tiny" volcano that never even produced a lava flow!

What supplies the power for volcanic eruptions anyway? Water. Yes, *water—superheated* water found in the underground liquid rock called magma. If some crack develops to release pressure, the superheated water flashes into steam, *generating colossal power*—power to blow islands apart, power that dwarfs mankind's nuclear arsenal. About ⅔ of what comes out of the average volcano is water vapor, what geologists call "juvenile water." How much water could be released by volcanic processes? Most evolutionists believe all the earth's oceans were filled by outgassing of volcanic water!

According to the Bible, the water for Noah's Flood was first released when the "fountains of the great deep burst forth" (Genesis 7:11). Imagine volcanoes many times more powerful than Mt. St. Helens, going off all over the world *at the same time*. That may help you begin to imagine catastrophe on a Biblical scale! And it's catastrophe on that Biblical scale that science *needs* to explain many of the physical features of our earth, such as the Grand Canyon.

The Grand Canyon

There's no doubt about it: the best place to see, study, and put together all these ideas about stacks of fossil-bearing rock is the Grand Canyon.

Grand Canyon is an awesome gash in the earth, running for about 200 miles (300 km) along the Colorado River in the northwest corner of Arizona. The Canyon is about a mile (1.6 km) deep, and about 10 miles (16 km) from north to south rims. The walls of the narrow, zig-zag inner gorge expose tilted and faulted Precambrian rock, while the walls of the outer and upper gorge are streaked with thick, colorful, horizontal bands of fossil-bearing rock, representing roughly the "bottom half" of the geologic column.

I once believed and taught, like so many others, that the rock layers in Grand Canyon represented stages in evolution laid down over vast eons of time. But, after leading over 15 week-long backpacking trips for university students through the Canyon and studying the rock layers and fossils close-up, I'm ready to stake the place out with Bible verses! What I once assumed was a record of a *lot of time*, now looks like evidence of a *lot of water* instead!

Actually, the Canyon seems to provide an excellent contrast between rocks laid down slowly and gradually on a local scale and those laid down rapidly and catastrophically on a colossal scale. Evolutionists have argued that fossil-bearing rocks were largely laid down in local floods and/or by rivers dumping sediments into lakes or seas. Those processes do build up sediment layers; the Mississippi River, the classic example, is continuing to build up its delta right before our eyes.

When the Mississippi is flowing full and fast (often after spring rains and snow melt), gravel is carried relatively far. Later, often during the drier summer season, the river slows, so that sand is dumped where gravel was, then silt on the sand. Such slow and gradual processes produce "lumpy" sediment layers that thicken and thin over short distances and *contain virtually no fossils*.

Actually, the Precambrian sedimentary rocks in the inner gorge probably *do* represent sediment laid down somewhat slowly and gradually. Like Mississippi delta deposits, these units thicken and thin, disappear and reappear, over short distances, and they contain very few fossils. They don't have the "layer-cake" appearance—deep and wide horizontal bands of fossil-rich rocks—characteristic of *rapid* flood deposits. Instead, they have the "swirl-cake" appearance—lumps of fossil-poor rock—like the sediment layers being produced at the mouth of the Mississippi River right now. To Biblical creationists/Flood geolgists, the Precambrian rocks at Grand Canyon look like pre-Flood or early Flood rocks formed by processes occurring like those today during the many centuries before the Flood.

But then the Flood came! There are still countless research projects to be done and questions to be answered, but let me share with you a simple model for the basic formation of Grand Canyon, that ties together most of the ideas we've been discussing. Please treat these ideas as a stimulus to thinking, not, by any means, as the last word on Grand Canyon.

Although most people relate the Flood to "forty days and forty nights of rain," the Bible says that the Flood *began* when "the fountains of the great deep burst forth." It seems that *most* of the water came from below, not from above.

Few people realize what a tremendous amount of water is found in molten rock (magma) trapped beneath the earth's surface! When a hole or crack develops in the solid rock capping the more liquid magma, the pressure release causes the super-super hot water to flash into steam, and "BOOM" we have an upward-outward rush of vapor, gas, dust, and ash, producing a volcanic explosion and/or an outpouring of liquid rock on the surface (lava)! A geologist looking for a way to start a worldwide flood could hardly come up with a better mechanism than breaking up the "fountains of the great deep!"

As the volcanic fountains opened up in what is now the Grand Canyon area, the colossally stupendous force just pushed the pre-Flood or early flood rock aside and tilted it up. The Precambrian rocks in the inner gorge are indeed cracked and tilted, and igneous intrusions cut across and between them, marking, I am suggesting, the beginning of Noah's Flood, recorded for our study.

The first Flood current in the area came with such tremendous force that it sheared off the tilted Precambrian rocks in virtually a straight line, producing the so-called "angular unconformity" diagrammed in Fig. 34. Science tells us that the tilt-and-shear could *not* have happened slowly and gradually. One of the tilted units (the reddish Hakatai Shale) is so soft and crumbly you can dig it out with your fingernails. Another is so incredibly hard (the Shinumo Quartzite) that researchers can barely knock off a piece with a hammer. Had the rocks been tilted up slowly and eroded gradually by rain drops and rivers, the crumbly rock would be all gone, leaving valleys, and the hard unit would stick up in ridges and hillocks. The two different rock types would result in a very wavy contact being formed at the angular unconformity between the tilted layers and the first horizontal unit, the Tapeats Sandstone. *Instead*, it looks as if the Flood current that eventually deposited the Tapeats came in with such titanic force that the hard and soft rocks were sheared off almost equally in a nearly straight line.

Actually, the Shinumo Quartzite is so hard that parts of it *do* occasionally stick up through the Tapeats. But the force of the Flood was so great that it broke off huge boulders of this incredibly hard rock, picked the boulders up, and carried them miles (kilometers) away before finally dropping them! Wow! Many devastating floods have been observed in historical times, but *none with such power*! So far as I know, there are no evolutionary ("uniformitarian") theories to explain how such huge boulders could be picked up and *slowly and gradually* moved by ordinary river and raindrop erosion! Even the Colorado River today, a classic example of strength and power, is unable to move lesser boulders downstream from the mouths of its side canyons.

Once the Flood got started, it began to deposit rock layers deep and wide and full of fossils, the "layer-cake" effect characteristic of floods—but on a scale far greater than anything recorded by human observers (except Noah and his family).

We do get some inkling of the kind of geological processes involved from the study of "underwater landslides" called turbidity currents. In 1929, an earthquake loosened sediment lying on the ocean floor off Newfoundland near the continental slope. The loosened sediment roared down the slope at freeway speeds, up to 60 miles or 100 kilometers per hour! How do we know? The dense, muddy slurry flowing along the bottom severed transatlantic telephone cables one after the other, so the time of travel could be calculated from the time telephone service stopped on each line. The roaring sediment spread out over the deep ocean's abyssal plain, covering an area of hundreds of square miles (kilometers) in a matter of *hours*! Many boulder flows, megabreccias, and other deposits which once mystified geologists are now interpreted, even by evolutionists, as huge layers deposited rapidly by turbidity currents. Some evolutionists estimate that perhaps 40% of the geologic column was formed by these stupendous flows!

When Biblical creationists/Flood geologists offer explanations for the rock layers in Grand Canyon, they appeal neither to Biblical authority (the Bible doesn't mention Grand Canyon!) nor to mystical or supernatural processes. They appeal, instead, directly to the evidence we can see, touch, and measure. That evidence seems to suggest that *processes we* do *understand*, like turbidity currents, explain what we see—except that the evidence *also* tells us that the scale was regional, continental, or even global, not just local.

Consider this dramatic statement from the secular (evolutionary) textbook by Levine that I have used with my college Earth Science classes.

> **Many channels on Mars dwarf our own Grand Canyon in size, and in order to form, would have required torrential floods so spectacular as to be hard to visualize by earth standards.**

Note three things: First, it's normal for a scientist to interpret channels like Grand Canyon in terms of flooding. Second, it's possible for a scientist to accept cataclysmic flooding on a planet that presently has little or no surface water. Third, a scientist can infer from the evidence left behind "torrential" and "spectacular" flooding on a scale far greater than anything ever recorded in scientific journals! Certainly there's nothing unscientific about inferring a colossal flood at Grand Canyon from the evidence on a planet (Earth) whose surface is drenched in water!

I've mentioned that, because of the overwhelming weight of scientific evidence, many evolutionists are now calling themselves neo-catastrophists. They want nothing to do with old-fashioned catastrophism (Noah's Flood!), but they agree that most layers of fossil-bearing rock were produced rapidly and broadly by flooding on a catastrophic scale, what Derek Ager compared to "short periods of terror" in the life of a soldier.

It's these short periods of terror, it seems, that caught plants and animals off guard, buried them too deeply and quickly for them to escape or to be obliterated by scavengers, and turned them into fossils. Clams and snails, for example, are not normally knocked dead and fossilized by a few sand grains or even by huge shifts of sand induced by hurricanes. But zillions were buried and fossilized, it seems, in the first overwhelming deposits of "Flood mud."

At Grand Canyon as around the world, the "first" or "deepest" layer to contain an abundance of fossil remains is called the Cambrian geologic system. As discussed earlier, these Cambrian "stones cry out" for Creation! Instead of a few simple life forms, hard to classify and apparently thrown together by time and chance, as an evolutionist might expect, we find a dazzling variety of complex life-forms, apparently well-designed to multiply after kind: clams, snails, lampshells, echinoderms, and the most complex of all invertebrates, the nautiloids ("shelled squids"), with an eye that sees the world as we do, and the trilobites, with their geometrically marvelous compound eyes.

But why should Cambrian deposits contain only (or *almost* only) the remains of sea creatures? A professor debating me in Australia put it this way: "If God created everything in six days, why don't we find mice with trilobites in Cambrian rocks?" My simple reply: "Because mice don't live on the sea floor." *Ecology, not evolution, is the key.* (He *then* said he meant his question only as a joke.)

Many people have the completely mistaken notion that the Biblical Flood covered the whole earth almost instantly, stirred everything up, and then suddenly dumped it all. Not at all! According to the Biblical record, Noah was in the Ark for over a year. It was about five months before "all the high mountains under the whole heavens" were covered, and it took several more months for the water to subside as "the mountains rose up and the valleys sank down" at the end of the Flood. As the Flood waters "slowly" rose over the earth, plants and animals were buried in a sort of ecologic series: sea-bottom creatures, near-shore forms, lowland plants and animals, then upland (with sea creatures deposited from bottom to top, as the sea eventually covered everything). Evolutionists and Flood geologists may agree that the fossil-bearing rocks were laid down in "short periods of terror," but Flood geologists see the "long periods of boredom" between layers as *minutes or months, not millions* of years!

Indeed, once the rock layers at Grand Canyon began to stack up, it seems they "forgot" all about "evolutionary time." In one small step (especially small with a heavy backpack!), a hiker can step right across "150 million years" of "missing evolutionary times"! I'm talking about the contact between the Muav and Redwall Limestones (Fig. 34).

The Muav is Cambrian (supposedly, "evolution stage 1"), while the Redwall is Mississippian or lower Carboniferous ("evolution stage 5"). If Grand Canyon is assumed to represent stages in evolution laid out for all to see, where are evolutionary stages 2, 3, and 4 (Ordovician, Silurian, and Devonian)? Evolutionists recognize that's a serious question. Grandparents can't have grandchildren without first having children, and plants and animals can't evolve directly from stage 1 to stage 5 without evolving through stages 2, 3, and 4 first. Everyone agrees that in any "chain of life," you can't skip generations!

Evolutionists recognize the problem of rock layers ("150 million years' worth") missing from Grand Canyon—*but* they also have a ready solution to the problem: erosion. Stage 2, 3, and 4 rocks really were deposited, they suggest, but they were uplifted and eroded away; then stage 5 rock (Mississippian Redwall) was laid down directly on top of stage 1 rock (Cambrian Muav). It's as if erosion tore out three chapters from the story of evolution!

That evolutionary argument is certainly logical and potentially correct. We see erosion erasing rock layers today, and we can infer that erosion also did so in the past. So evolutionists went looking for evidence of erosion, but they were honest enough to admit that they did not find it, at least not on a sufficient scale.

When a rock layer is eroded slowly and gradually by streams and rivers, as discussed earlier, an irregular surface is produced. When sediment later accumulates on this surface and hardens, the wavy contact line produced is called a *disconformity*, and often old stream beds may be identified along its surface. That's *not* what we find at the Redwall/Muav (Mississippian/Cambrian) contact. Over hundreds of miles of exposure in and out of various side canyons, the two rock layers are in smooth, horizontal contact. There are occasional small erosional dips called Temple Butte Devonian, but the regional picture is clear: it looks like one rock layer was deposited directly on top of the other with very little time break. According to the evidence, those 150 million years never existed at all![48]

If there were strong evidence for 150 million years of erosion, geologists would call the contact a *disconformity*. Because the evidence suggests, instead, smooth, continuous deposition with little time break, the contact *should* be called a *conformity*. But admitting a 150-million-year "hole" in evolutionary theory would be far too difficult for most evolutionists, so they use the contact term we discussed earlier: *paraconformity*. Flood geologists just accept the evidence as it stands: *no* 150 million years. But evolution requires 150 million years at that point. Hence, the term "paraconformity" is offered, *not* as a solution to the problem of all that missing time, but as a label for a problem to be solved by future research.

Evolutionists *believe* that *other evidence* for evolution is so strong that paraconformities can be regarded as just minor glitches in an otherwise convincing story. That's exactly how *I* dealt with "minor mysteries" when *I* believed and taught evolution. There's certainly nothing wrong with that approach, but, note, that it's an act of *faith*, not science. Flood geologists can simply *accept* the directly observable evidence for rapid, continuous deposition, the more scientific choice at this point.

There's further evidence to encourage Flood geologists to think that they have made the correct scientific choice. If individual sediment layers were hardened, uplifted, eroded, then covered again with water, it's likely that the lower hardened layers would crack in a pattern different from cracks formed in layers above them, and produced and moved millions of years later. In other words, there should be "buried faults," cracks through one layer not continuing into the layer above. But there are virtually no buried faults above the Precambrian in the Canyon. There are faults, all right, but they cut continuously through the *whole sequence* of Paleozoic layers present (Cambrian, Mississippian, Pennsylvanian, and Permian), *not just part of it.* That evidence suggests the whole "layer cake" was formed rapidly and continuously, without a major break in time—just as you would expect from understanding Grand Canyon in terms of what the Bible says about Noah's Flood.

But then we come to the Coconino Sandstone. Above the Redwall are several other major layers (Supai Group, Hermit Shale, Coconino Sandstone, Toroweap Formation, and Kaibab Limestone, as shown in Fig. 34). All these were obviously laid down as water-borne sediment (i.e., flood deposits)—except the Coconino. The Coconino is a

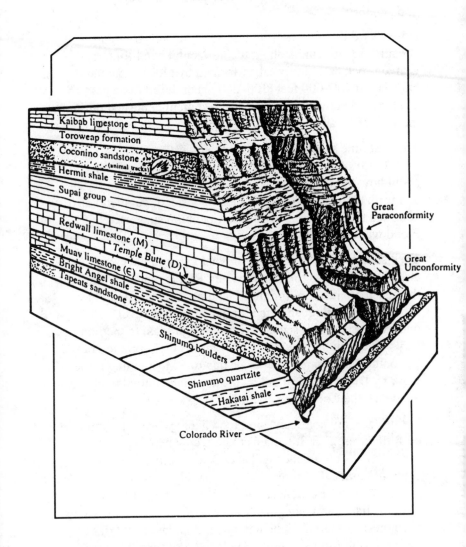

Figure 34. Grand Canyon: a *lot of time*, or a *lot of water*? . . .a record of *evolution*? Or of the *Biblical* outline of history: **Creation, Corruption, Catastrophe, Christ!**

cross-bedded sandstone usually interpreted as a huge desert dune deposit.

Now why did I have to bring that up? I've been trying to encourage you to think about the horizontal bands of Grand Canyon rock as a "layer cake" formed by global flooding. How could 400–600 feet (100–200 m) of desert dune get sandwiched between two layers of sediment deposited during the year of Noah's Flood?

The first time someone asked me that question, I didn't know what to say. Admitting the problem, I sputtered something about how the Bible talks about a great wind that blew back and forth over the earth as the Flood subsided, but then I also admitted that the layers above the Coconino suggested the Flood was still depositing.

Then somebody reminded me of what I should have known already: dunes also form underwater. Ripple marks in sand at the beach are just "mini-dunes," and my students and I have actually watched much bigger dunes form and travel underwater while on scuba dives (in rough seas) to the Florida Keys. The weight of evidence now favors the formation of the Coconino as an *underwater dune deposit*. Most telling is the work by Dr. Leonard Brand on the abundant animal trackways for which the Coconino is famous.[49]

In this case, my confidence in Flood geology was confirmed by further research. It remains to be seen whether the evolutionist's confidence will *ever* be encouraged by further study of paraconformities. There are surely many other questions to be researched, but the weight of evidence we have available now (and that's as far as science can go) seems to suggest strongly that the horizontal rock layers at Grand Canyon were formed rapidly, *not* by a lot of time, but by a *lot of water instead*!

But if the rock layers got stacked up under water, we have another problem. The North Rim of Grand Canyon is now over 8000 feet. (over 2500 m) above sea level. How did that happen? How did the rock layers end up far above sea level, and where did that big gash, the Canyon itself that cuts through all those layers, come from?

The Bible tells us that at the end of the Flood "the mountains rose up and the valleys sank down." An evolutionist friend of mine once told me that the best evidence for the Creation/Corruption/Catastrophe model he knew was that *any land existed at all on the earth.* If our planet had spun down from a gas cloud, he said, the outer layers would consist of basaltic ocean crust (density $3.5 g/cm^3$), covered by a concentric layer of granite ($3.0 g/cm^3$), the whole thing covered by over 2 miles (3 km) of water (density $1.0 g/cm^3$)! He said it looked as if "someone with big hands" (the closest he could come to saying "God") took the granite and shoved it up into a pile to form the dry land. Then he added that the "guy with big hands" was also smart enough to thin the basalt under the granite piles to maintain the earth in gravitational balance (isostasy) so that it wouldn't fracture as it rotated.

Perhaps God did use supernatural means to raise the land after the Flood as He did on the third day of the creation week. Or perhaps He used secondary means not yet discovered. A Biblical creationist/Flood geologist would never want to rule out God's direct supernatural intervention (our salvation and resurrection depend on it!), but neither would he or she appeal to supernatural processes unless logic or the evidence clearly pointed in that direction. Actually, neither creationist nor evolutionist is satisfied with present models for "upwarp" and "downwarp," moving big chunks of land above and below sea level.

However the land was raised, the next question is this: Where did the Canyon itself come from? The Flood may have *stacked* the rock like a giant layer cake, but what *cut* the cake?

One thing for sure: the Colorado River did not do it. The Colorado River starts about 12,000 feet. (ca. 3,500 m) up in the Rocky Mountains of western Colorado. By the time it gets to the Grand Canyon area, it's at about 5,000 feet. (1,500 m). And that's the problem. Grand Canyon is definitely *not* a lowland valley. The North Rim of the Canyon is over 8,000 feet. (2,500 m) high! For the Colorado River to carve the Canyon, it would first have to hack its way half a mile (over 700 m) uphill! Water just doesn't do that, especially when there's the opportunity to flow downhill in a different direction. For this and several other reasons, even evolutionary geologists no longer believe that the River *slowly* cut the Canyon over 60 million years.

The Kaibab upwarp (monocline) through which the Canyon is cut seems to have dammed up a great deal of water. It is possible to map the outlines of a giant "fossil lake" that once covered parts of Arizona, Colorado, and Utah. Since there seems to be no renewable source for such a vast amount of water, it may have been "leftover" Flood water trapped as the mountains rose and valleys sank.

Then the dam broke! The Grand Canyon area is crisscrossed with earthquake fault lines, so it might have been some sort of rift or fault that tore a breach in the dam. The water impounded by the dam would have rushed through the crack, probably cutting the essential features of the Canyon very rapidly indeed. The Colorado River (which is not even able to move the boulders at the mouths of its side canyons) is just a modest trickle caught in the twists and turns where the dam was breached. *The Canyon came first; the River came second.*[50]

Now, if the evidence is as clear and simple as I'm suggesting it is, then even evolutionary geologists who were totally unwilling even to consider my Biblical conclusions could at least accept the individual points as scientifically logical—and they do.

Consider Harlan Bretz. For years and years, he studied the "Channeled Scablands" of eastern Washington, a area of 15,000 miles.^{2} (40,000 km^2). It looks as if a giant, braided stream cut channels up to 900 feet. (250 m) deep in hard basaltic lava (much harder to cut than most of the Grand Canyon layers). Bretz postulated that a tongue of glacial ice blocked off what we now call the Columbia River near Spokane, damming up a huge body of water called glacial Lake Missoula. Then the ice-dam broke. And, according to Bretz, the stupendous drainage from that lake cut the essential features of those channels 900 feet. (250 m) deep over 15,000 miles^2 (40,000 km^2) in—one or two million years?— no, in "a day or two." That's the conclusion presented by the U. S. Geological Survey (USGS) in its phamplet[51] "The Channeled Scablands: the Story of the Great Spokane Flood."

At first, the "slow and gradual" school of evolutionary thought ("uniformitarians") laughed Bretz to scorn. But after examining his evidence, a team of geologists decided Bretz was right after all, and they gave him geology's highest award, the Penrose Medal. In accepting the award, Bretz said that his greatest contribution to geology was reviving the idea that great catastrophes have shaped the physical features of the earth ("neo-catastrophism").[52]

Less dramatic in scale, but directly and awesomely visible, was an eruption of Mt. St. Helens. We have described the first eruption in May of 1980, as the force of water flashing to steam blew the top 1300 feet. (400 m) off the north side of the volcano. More to the immediate point was the explosion in June of 1982. The heat generated from that explosion melted frozen mud, producing a mud flow that filled up the North Fork of the Toutle River. The smoke cleared five days later to reveal that the mud flow had been eroded into a zig-zag main channel with many sharply tapered side canyons. Horizontal bands of sediment, some thick, and some exceedingly fine, lined the walls of the newly formed canyon. Right before our

Washington State Dept. Natural Resources

Dr. Steve Austin

Figure 35. The eruption of Mt. St. Helens in 1982 formed a ¼₀ "scale model" of Grand Canyon in just 5 days. Other effects observed at Mt. St. Helens dramatically and visibly supported Creation/Flood geologist theories about the rapid formation of coal, polystrates, and sediment banding. (There is an excellent video by Dr. Steven Austin available from Master Books.)

eyes, a small volcano (which never even produced a lava flow) had stacked up horizontal bands of sediment, and cut channels through it, *forming a ¹/₄₀th size "scale model" of Grand Canyon in just five days*! All sorts of features once thought to take millions of years of time were formed, instead, by a lot of water in just five days! And my wife and I got to see it on a dizzying flight down the length of that "Little Grand Canyon." (See Austin video,[53] Morris,[54] and Fig. 35.)

Although very dramatic, both the Channeled Scablands and Mt. St. Helens are quite modest events compared to the epic geologic work that would have been done by a Global Flood like that described in the Bible.

At least the worldwide evidence is now so clear that even evolutionists are talking about worldwide catastrophes. The most highly touted is supposed to be an asteroid impact that wiped out the dinosaurs and a host of other life forms. Scientists have calculated that if an ocean were hit by an asteroid about 6 miles (10 km) across (and several that size pass near earth's orbit!), a wave of water would slosh over all the continents and bring nearly instant destruction on an unimaginable scale!

The Bible doesn't say whether God used secondary agents, such as an asteroid impact, to trigger the Flood. Either way, it's encouraging to see that evolutionists recognize the evidence that points toward global catastrophe. Indeed, some evolutionist now believe the earth has suffered *multiple* global catastrophes, and I mentioned that others even see evidence of colossal flooding on Mars, a planet that presently has no significant surface water!

The asteroid catastrophes some evolutionists postulate are dramatic, and so is the Biblical narrative, as it tells how "all the high mountains under the whole heavens" were once covered with water. If that were so, we ought to find billions of dead things buried in rock layers laid down by water all over the earth. Grab your pick and shovel and go looking, and what do you find? *Billions of dead things buried in rock layers laid down by water all over the earth*! Right up to sea creatures fossilized in the high Himalayas, it looks like the scientific evidence in God's world encourages us to trust the Bible as God's Word!

Sometimes, I imagine a geologist who has spent 20 years roaming through Grand Canyon. Finally, he decides to take a break and hike up to the rim. There, on a park bench, he finds a Bible. As he opens it and reads the first few chapters, he jumps excitedly to his feet. "Eureka! I've found it! That's what I've been seeing here in Grand Canyon!"

1. "Now I know why the first forms of life to leave an abundance of fossil remains are so complex and varied, and classify into groups like we have today. They were created well-designed to multiply after their kinds."

2. "Now I know why the 'geologic column' shows a decline in variety, even extinction, for so many groups. We're not looking at a record of evolutionary progress, but a record of death—a Corruption of the world God had created all very good. Grand Canyon is really a vast, open graveyard."

3. "Now I know how fossils were preserved, how the Precambrian rocks were tilted up and sheared off, how the huge Tapeats boulders were moved great distances, why 150-million mythical years are missing at the great paraconformity, how trackways were preserved in the Coconino, and why the Colorado River is trapped in the sharp curves of the Canyon. We're not looking at a record of a lot of time, but of a lot of water—the tremendous worldwide Catastrophe of Noah's Flood!"

4. "Now I know I can look to Christ to raise me to new life. Nobody could ever have survived the awesome destruction of the world we see reflected at Grand Canyon. And if Christ could save Noah from the Flood, He can save me from death, too!"

When I started working on my doctoral minor in geology, I really thought my study would make it very hard to accept the simple truths and promises in the Bible. My excellent professors all believed evolution, but what I learned about *fossils made it hard to believe evolution and very easy to believe what the Bible teaches about Creation, Corruption, Catastrophe, and Christ!*

We find evidence of Creation not only in the design and complexity of the "first" fossils found of each group, but also in the wonderfully constructed "language" of DNA; in the intricate way a baby develops in his or her mother's womb according to the plan fully presented at conception; in the similarities that point to "common Creator," not common ancestry, in classification; in marvelously interdependent adaptations, like those of the woodpecker; in the incredible variability, like all the human skin colors, stored in the first parents of each created kind.

We find evidence of Corruption, the way God's Creation was ruined by man's self-centered arrogance, not only in the death, decline, and extinction seen in all the fossil groups, but also in the effects of mutations producing disease, disease organisms, and other defects, and in the struggle to the death that is an essential part of Darwinian selection.

Evidence of a great Catastrophe, like the world-wide Flood described for Noah's time, is clear from the billions of dead things buried as fossils, extinction, rapid formation of huge sediment layers by turbidity currents, polystratic fossils that cut through many rock layers without evidence of falling over or rotting, paraconformities (vast amounts of supposed evolutionary time missing without evidence or erosion), the tilting and shearing and boulder flows in Grand Canyon, etc., etc., etc.

All the above can be inferred directly from the scientific evidence, although it's the Bible that really puts these together in a pattern of meaning. Evolution is based on genetics that have never been observed and fossils that have never been found. The Bible is supported by laws of heredity we put into practice everyday and on thousands of tons of fossils buried in rock layers laid down by water all over the earth.

In short, *evolution is a faith that the facts have failed*. **Biblical Christianity is a faith that fits the facts.**

As I told you in the beginning, I didn't always believe that. It took me three years of trying to *"prove"* evolution to two colleagues, professors of chemistry and biology, before I saw that the scientific evidence available *disproves* the traditional view of evolution taught as "fact" to millions of young people worldwide.

Does that mean I've *proved* Creation? Not at all. Contrary to a popular misconception, scientists can only *disprove* or *support* a theory, never prove it. As every working scientist knows, you can never tell when some new discovery will shift support to a competing theory. People (including scientists!) are finite, limited by space and time. As finite creatures, we must live by faith; there is no other choice.

But we *can choose* the object of our faith. We can put our faith in our own opinions or the words of "experts," as I did through my first several years of teaching university biology. Or we can put our faith in the Word of the Living God, who stands outside our limits of space and time. Only God can tell us what is truly true, now and forever.

The difference between evolution and the Bible is certainly evident when we look back at where we've come from, but the difference is even *greater* when we consider where we're going! I once let my students watch two well-known evolutionists on a TV talk show that aired during class time. The audience wanted to know, "What does the future hold?" The fossil expert said the fate of essentially every species is extinction, and that mankind, too, would someday become extinct. The audience broke into applause, although I've never figured out what's so wonderful about becoming extinct! When they asked the evolutionist astronomer about the future, his reply was that one day the sun would expand and all life on earth would be burned to death, and again the audience broke into applause.

However, the Bible offers a more lively hope! The same God in Christ who created us, is the same God who did not turn away from us when we turned away from Him. Indeed, Jesus Christ paid the penalty for our rebellion, died to conquer death, and rose again to raise *those who believe* to new life in Him.

Jesus Himself asked, "How can you believe me when I tell you heavenly things if you don't believe me when I tell you earthly things?" Science shows us we *can* trust the Bible when it tells us earthly things about Creation, Corruption, and Catastrophe. That encourages us to trust the "Fourth C," Jesus Christ, for the promise of a new and abundant life now and forever, and of a "new heavens and new earth," where God will "wipe away every tear" and restore the Creation to the way He made it for us in the beginning: a garden of Eden, a garden of Delight. Then once again, "the wolf also shall dwell with the lamb. . . and a little child shall lead them. . . . They shall not hurt nor destroy in all my holy mountain, for the earth shall be full of the knowledge of the Lord as the waters cover the sea" (Isaiah 11:6–9).

It's a wonderful, wonderful story, full of love and meaning for each person on earth. And *what we see in God's world encourages us to trust the Bible as God's Word.* Then those wonderful promises can be ours, *guaranteed by the power of the Lord God, Maker of heaven and earth,* the God of all people, all times, and all places. If God made us, we can trust Him to make us *anew*! Won't you choose to trust Him now?

The study of science offers *more* than science lessons. There are spiritual lessons as well.

End Notes

1   Kelly, Thomas (producer). *Puzzle of the Ancient Wing*. Canadian Broadcasting Corporation: "Man Alive" television series. 1981.

2   Raup, David. "Conflicts Between Darwin and Palentology." *Field Museum of Natural History Bulletin*. January 1979.

3   Raup, David. "Geology and Creationism." *Field Museum of Natural History Bulletin*. March 1983.

4   Barnhart, Walter R. *A Critical Evaluation of the Phylogeny of the Horse*. Master's thesis. Santee, CA: Institute for Creation Research. 1987.

5   Gish, Duane T. *Evolution: The Challenge of the Fossil Record*. Colorado Springs: Master Books. 1986.

6   Eldredge, Niles. As quoted in the *Sunday Mail*. Brisbane, Australia, September 14, 1986.

7   Taylor, Paul S. *The Great Dinosaur Mystery*. Elgin, IL: David C. Cook, Pub. 1989.

8   Denton, Michael. *Evolution: A Theory in Crisis*. London: Burnett Books. 1985.

9   Wilford, John N. "Feathered Dinosaur or Real Bird." *New York Times*, February 5, 1993.

10 Taylor, Ian. *In the Minds of Men*. 3rd ed. Toronto: TFE Pub. 1992.

11 Ostrom, John H. "Bird Flight: How Did It Begin?" *American Scientist*, January/February 1979.

12 Gish, Duane T. *The Challenge of the Fossil Record*. Colorado Springs: Master Books. 1986.

13 Bliss, Richard B., Gary E. Parker, and Duane T. Gish. *Fossils: Key to the Present*. Colorado Springs: Master Books. Two Models Creation-Evolution Series. 1980.

14 Gould, Stephen Jay. "The Return of Hopeful Monsters." *Natural History*, June/July 1977.

15 Adler, Jerry and John Carey. "Is Man a Subtle Accident?" *Newsweek*, November 3, 1980.

16 Kelly, Thomas (producer). *Puzzle of the Ancient Wing*. Canadian Broadcasting Corporation: "Man Alive" television series. 1981.

17 Osborn, Henry. "The Evolution of Human Races." *Natural History*, April, 1980. (Reprinted from *Natural History*, January/February 1926).

18 Gould, Stephen Jay. "The Brain Appraisers." *Science Digest*, September 1981.

19 Gould, Stephen Jay. "Smith Woodward's Folly." *New Scientist*, April 5, 1979.

20 Lubenow, Marvin. *Bones of Contention*. Grand Rapids: Baker Books. 1992.

21 Zihlman, Adrienne, and Jerold Lowenstein. "False Start of the Human Parade." *Natural History*, August/September. 1979.

22 Simons, Elwyn. "Just a Nasty Little Thing." As quoted in *Time*, February 18, 1980.

23 Oxnard, Charles E. "Human Fossils: New View of Old Bones." *American Biology Teacher*, May 1979.

24 Lemonick, Michael. "How Man Began." *Time*, March 14, 1994.

25 Oxnard, Charles E. "Human Fossils: New View of Old Bones." *American Biology Teacher*, May 1979.

26 Lubenow, Marvin. *Bones of Contention*. Grand Rapids: Baker Books. 1992.

27 Leakey, Mary D. "Footprints in the Ashes of Time." *National Geographic*, April 1979.

28 Leakey, Mary D. "Happy Trail for Three Hominids." *Science News*, February 9, 1980.

29 Adler, Jerry and John Carey. "Is Man a Subtle Accident?" *Newsweek*, November 3, 1980.

30 Lewin, Roger. "Evolutionary Theory Under Fire." *Science*, November 21, 1980.

31 Gould, Stephen Jay, and Niles Eldredge. "Punctuated Equilibria: the Tempo and Mode of Evolution Reconsidered." *Paleobiology*, June/July 1977.

32 Stanley, Steven M. "Darwin Done Over." *The Sciences*, October 1981.

33 Lewin, Roger. "Evolutionary Theory Under Fire." *Science*, November 21, 1980.

34 Denton, Michael. *Evolution: A Theory in Crisis*. London: Burnett Books. 1985.

35 Threlkeld, Richard. CBS Television "Sunday Morning," November 23, 1980.

36 Folger, Tim. "The Biggest Flood." *Discover*, January 1994. (pages 36, 38).

37 Weier, T. E., C. R Stocking, and M. G. Barbour. *Botany*. 5th ed. New York: John Wiley and Sons. 1974.

38 Gould, Stephen Jay. "Is a New and General Theory of Evolution Emerging?" *Paleobiology*, Winter 1980.

39 Nevins, Stuart E. "Origin of Coal." *Acts and Facts* "Impact" Series No. 41. El Cajon: Institute for Creation Research. November. 1976.

40 Austin, Steven A. Depositional Environment of the Kentucky No. 12 Coal Bed (Middle Pennsylvanian) of Western Kentucky, With Special Reference to the Origin of Coal Lithotypes. Dissertation. Pennsylvania State University (University Microfilms International). Ann Arbor, MI. 1979. Page 390. Order No. 8005972.

41 Austin, Steven A. *Mt. St. Helens* (video). Santee, CA: Institute for Creation Research. 1993.

42 Taylor, Ian. *In the Minds of Men*. 3rd ed. Toronto: TFE Pub. 1992.

43 Gould, Stephen Jay. "Evolution's Erratic Pace." *Natural History*, May 1977.

44 Ager, Derek V. "The Nature of the Fossil Record." *Proceedings of the Geological Association* 87(2). Pages 131-159. 1976.

45 Sheven, Jachim. Interviewed in "Meet Mr. Living Fossils." *Creation Ex Nihilo*, March-May 1993.

46 Raup, David. "The Revolution in Evolution." *World Book Science Year 1980*.

47 Austin, Steven A. *Mt. St. Helens* (video). Santee, CA: Institute for Creation Research. 1993.

48 Snelling, Andrew. "The Case of the 'Missing' Geologic Time." *Creation Ex Nihilo*, June-August 1992.

49 Snelling, Andrew, and Steven A. Austin. "Startling Evidence of Noah's Flood in a Grand Canyon Sandstone." *Creation Ex Nihilo*, December 1992-February 1993.

50 Austin, Steven A. (editor). *Grand Canyon: Monument to Catastrophe*. Santee, CA: Institute for Creation Research. 1994.

51 U. S. Geological Survey. *The Channeled Scablands of Eastern Washington—The Geologic Story of the Great Spokane Flood*. 1976.

52 Bretz, Harlan. As quoted in "GSA Medals and Awards." *GSA (Geological Society of America) News and Information*, March 1980.

53 Austin, Steven A. *Mt. St. Helens* (video). Santee, CA: Institute for Creation Research. 1993.

54 Morris, John. *The Young Earth*. Colorado Springs: Master Books. 1994.